T0300634

44 Poems on Being with Each Other

Also by Pádraig Ó Tuama

Kitchen Hymns
Poetry Unbound: 50 Poems to Open Your World
Feed the Beast
Being Here
Borders and Belonging (with Glenn Jordan)
Daily Prayer with the Corrymeela Community
In the Shelter
Sorry for Your Troubles
Readings from the Books of Exile

44 Poems on Being with Each Other

A *Poetry Unbound* Collection

Pádraig Ó Tuama

W. W. NORTON & COMPANY

Independent Publishers Since 1923

First published in Great Britain and Canada in 2025 by
Canongate Books, Ltd.

Copyright © 2025 by Pádraig Ó Tuama
First American Edition 2025

Poetry Unbound is a trademark of On Being

O
BEING

For information about permission to reproduce selections from this book,
write to Permissions, W. W. Norton & Company, Inc., 500 Fifth Avenue,
New York, NY 10110

For information about special discounts for bulk purchases, please
contact W. W. Norton Special Sales at specialsales@wwnorton.com or
800-233-4830

Manufacturing by Lakeside Book Company

ISBN: 978-1-324-08616-1

W. W. Norton & Company, Inc.
500 Fifth Avenue, New York, NY 10110
www.wwnorton.com

W. W. Norton & Company Ltd.
15 Carlisle Street, London W1D 3BS

10 9 8 7 6 5 4 3 2 1

Contents

To Peter Coleman and Leah Doyle, with thanks and love

To Krista Tippett, with delight and celebration

The very foundation of interhuman discourse is
misunderstanding.

Jacques Lacan

Introduction

In the space of the year it's taken to write this book I've met a lot of strangers, sat in a lot of meetings, and read a lot of things. I've been alone, with friends; I've wanted to join some groups and wanted to leave some others. I've hurt. I've been hurt. I cried on a train. I burst out laughing at a text message. I panicked when someone close to me got a diagnosis, then tried to de-panic myself. I've been late because the birdsong was beautiful. I broke a bone and had a long conversation with a medic who told me I'd have been a terrible doctor. Out of the blue, someone from my past reemerged. I've wondered about my health while worrying about the health of others. I've watched the news about Ukraine and Gaza with horror. I argued with politicians while drinking morning tea. I gave money. I gave attention. I was alert. I was lazy. I've been awake more hours than I wanted. I slept well. I slept badly. I gave gifts. I refused others.

I've inhabited the homes of friends, strangers and acquaintances for months at a time, drinking from their cups, looking at their photos. I stopped in front of posters displaying the names and photos of kidnapped Israelis. I was the celebrant at a friend's wedding, and couldn't have been happier. I heard from an old lover. I've spoken Irish with some people, French with others, and wished I could remember the German word for world-sadness. I've judged my own body and judged my curiosity about the bodies of others. I've separated and I've joined. I've feared. I've introduced people to each other and watched their friendships flourish.

And that's not all. I've seen life and death. I've seen hope and horror. I've seen grief, gladness, good food and greed. I've read articles, novels, headlines, text messages, letters, food labels, whiskey descriptions, departures information and station signs. A broken bone was not enough; I cracked another.

What happens in a life? All of this, and more. From the memorable to the mundane, moments appear that ask for our attention; we give it, we move on, we remember some events and forget many others. The Irish word *file* translates as 'poet' but also as 'seer'. I'm hesitant to imagine that poets have special insight, or particular powers of perception. We don't. We just work damned hard to see, remember, write, see again and write more. So a poem is an act of noticing. What does it see? It sees forward and backward. It sees the futures that probably won't happen. A poem understands the past has a life of its own, and is both patient and impatient with lament. It can contain rage and hunger, it can protest at the state of the world, and plot the low plod toward resented compromise. Poems are recipes for happiness and prayers for when no other prayers will do. They record what's unfolded, and also what's been hidden in the folds. Poems confess, apologise, ask forgiveness, ask for mercy, ask for time, ask for space, ask to be read again, and ask for attention. A poem might be addressed to someone who'll never read it – be they estranged, or uninterested, or dead – but the address is to *you* and *you* can be anyone.

*

Poems see all kinds of things, but the ones gathered here are about being with each other. When we are with each other, anything can happen, and it has. I know you know this. Just think about what happened yesterday. Or this morning. Or last week. Or last year. I've had longstanding unease with the word 'family'. I come from a good one, but too many years hearing *family values* – from priests and politicians and many in between – left me with the distinct impression that my life was considered some kind of threat to those values. Why? Too gay, I suppose. But that's not the only reason people find themselves feeling alienated from the idea of the family. While I understand the usage of the nuclear family – from nucleus, a little unit – the adjective also makes me think about bombs. This collection of poems explores fusion and fission: familiar familiars; the explosions and fireworks that happen when people are in proximity with people; the love so pure it breaks you; the pull of attachment and the draw of resistance. We all know all about this; it happens in and between us. What happens when we are with each other? What happens in the aftermath? What do we do then? We use language. We make. We look. We hope. We speak. We listen. We change, in all kinds of ways.

The forty-four poems in this *Poetry Unbound* collection are interested in the energy that occurs between people. Strangers. Lovers. Friends. Colleagues. (I'm going to stop before I make yet another list.) Chen Chen describes parenting his parents as they learn – or try to learn – how to acknowledge their son's life. Some of us finally end up in families that are so good we can hardly bear it, and Eugenia Leigh learns lessons from a beetle as she tries to cajole herself to return to her home. Some of us fight in our families, and the fights reveal truths about fear. Philip Metres's neighbours wanted to cut down a beloved tree, and the tension spread within the house. Is a neighbour an enemy? Not usually. Sometimes. In the absence of enemies we are capable of inventing them, and C.P. Cavafy has a warning from 1898 for those of us who rely on fantasised foes. If you're lucky, occasionally you'll feel a 'brutal pull' that complicates your resistance, propelling you into an unexpected orbit. Dorianne Laux knows all about that and has written a prescription for your trajectory. Change happens, and with change comes change. Caroline Bird reflects on her childhood: 'On behalf of my younger self, I apologise / to my parents' she says, and how many of us have yearned for apologies: to make them, to hear them, to feel them, to refute them, to move beyond them? The space between people is sometimes minimal, sometimes vast. Sasha taqʷšəblu LaPointe speaks of a disappeared brother, Langston Hughes loved his friend but 'he went away from me.' Benjamin Gucciardi facilitates classrooms of boys in discussing their lives, and often that's a trudge, but sometimes something happens that fills the space with love. What happened to you? Today, I mean. What has occurred that is asking for your attention? Did you discover something new to worry about? Laura Villareal imagines her worries as parents with little worry-babies of their own. Did you have a moment where empathy arrived in your life like a complicated guest? Robert Hayden had that too, and considers his rough father with generosity and self-recrimination. Were you finally happy? Wendy Cope understands: she cut an orange and divided it with friends. Did you have a moment of insight, in which the hostilities of a group were understood as the yearnings for art and voice? Mark Turcotte writes a letter just for you. What happened as you watched the news? Mosab Abu Toha's poem remembers a Palestinian elder statesman, lamenting the lack of a kitchen window, a kitchen wall, a kitchen plant, a kitchen. Are you facing the end of things? In war, or life? Jim Moore faces those losses: his wife, his friends, himself. He offers wisdom, fear and love to hold you together. Did someone long dead turn up? Of course they did; *familiar* can mean ghost as well as family, and death makes demands on the imaginations of the living. Kandace Siobhan Walker sees her dead grandmother walking down a street in London, wearing purple, squeezing unripe mangoes in the fruit stalls.

What else happened today? Have you found yourself at the edge of things? Michael Wasson has, and he takes the voice of his late mother to speak back to himself. Did your feelings threaten to overwhelm you? Nick Flynn makes a long list of his and then crosses it out, making and unmaking, and showing us what to do with chaos, blame and creativity. Tiana Clark makes a list too; but she takes a bath instead. Did you shower yourself with rage? Were you remembering the bastard family who did the terrible thing? Zuzanna Ginczanka's poem of truth, revenge, power and message from beyond the horror of the Holocaust will make you listen to your language, and consider how it should be directed. Nico Amador comes to help, asking you to ponder whether the gods you turn to are gods of war or of wonder. And Patricia Smith looks at such a god, a teacher, for whom she wanted to live and learn and grow and shine.

What happens in a poem? The same as happens in a life: all kinds of things. Here are forty-four poems on being with each other. My hope is that you can be with yourself. I know it's not always easy. Lucille Clifton's declaration of herself will make and break you. Valencia Robin will look – with you – at the things you said that perhaps you shouldn't have said. She'll offer sharp understanding mixed with curiosity: *where did that language come from?* Thomas Lux was filled with a yearning too beautiful to satisfy, and his aching will ache you, and, with him, you'll remember that desire is sometimes its own reward. Our lives are so busy, so filled with demands. Even if we want to be good to each other, it's hard to know how to be good to each other. What helps? Being grounded. Joy Harjo will ask you what the land says. We make our way with each other by making phone calls, and, with Safia Elhillo, by praising the friends whose lives we know by heart. We make it through by seeking ways to change, hurt though that might, and see ourselves as more than just our wounds. That's not easy; Kai Cheng Thom's words help, as do Mary Oliver's difficult dreams. We turn the gaze upon ourselves, trying to jolt ourselves awake, alive. Molly Twomey, together with her dad and a nurse, will make you consider what your work in the world is: when to help, when to stop. John Lee Clark will deepen your questions, and query the ground of assumption you stand on. It's necessary. It's funny-but-not-funny. And it's true.

Along the way there is delight. Surprise. Raptors. Sketches. Children. Forgiveness. Compassion. Lament. Swimming. Tattoos. Parties. Love. A child will stare at you, and an old shame will rise in you. It's terrible. Andy Jackson knows all about it. He prescribes near-nakedness, water, conversation and solidarity with those who matter. I do not know what a human being is, but – like you – I know some things about us. Wisława Szymborska's statements about the human condition open this collection. Are we capable of change? Are we all brutal in the end? She doesn't answer, but she asks, and the poems that follow continue her inquiry. In her seeing, the human person is many things: complicated, just like all of us. 'The human condition' is a hungry beast – it's no wonder we struggle to be together. Reminding ourselves how demanding, delightful, terrible and tender we can be helps. Not much is easy: hold on; read poetry; be poetry to each other.

A story of Jericho Brown's brings the collection to a close: a man is visited by a lover and a brother. The man is in need. Neither the lover nor the brother is used to being with each other, but it is their surprising and mutual concern for the man that brings them together. Someone feels like they're weak, in pain, judged; but something else is happening too: unexpected gatherings of people who'd otherwise not coincide. Familiarity where hostility had previously bred. Curiosity unfolding our lives. Mutual attention. Something said. Something heard. Something made. Something growing. Something new.

Pádraig Ó Tuama, 2024

Studying group behaviour in my twenties, I learnt that *Most people do what seems reasonable to them, most of the time.* I liked it. I still do. I think it holds some truth.

On a second look, the phrase has another truth: *Some people will do what seems unreasonable to them, some of the time.* I don't like this. I wish I didn't believe it. It, too, holds truth.

Poetry is a human art, and therefore is as capable of and as susceptible to error and manipulation as any one of us is. I would rather this not be the case. But it is the case. What to do? Ask. Read. Ask again. Look. Learn. Try to change.

A Word on Statistics
Wisława Szymborska

Out of every hundred people

those who always know better:
fifty-two.

Unsure of every step:
nearly all the rest.

Ready to help,
as long as it doesn't take long:
forty-nine.

Always good,
because they cannot be otherwise:
four – well, maybe five.

Able to admire without envy:
eighteen.

Led to error
by youth (which passes):
sixty, plus or minus.

Those not to be messed with:
forty and four.

Living in constant fear
of someone or something:
seventy-seven.

Capable of happiness:
twenty-some-odd at most.

Harmless alone,
turning savage in crowds:
more than half, for sure.

Cruel
when forced by circumstances:
it's better not to know
not even approximately.

Wise in hindsight:
not many more
than wise in foresight.

Getting nothing out of life but things:
thirty
(although I would like to be wrong).

Doubled over in pain,
without a flashlight in the dark:
eighty-three,
sooner or later.

Those who are just:
quite a few at thirty-five.

But if it takes effort to understand:
three.

Worthy of empathy:
ninety-nine.

Mortal:
one hundred out of one hundred –
a figure that has never varied yet.

Translation by Joanna Trzeciak Huss

In nineteen stanzas, Wisława Szymborska's 'A Word on Statistics' offers eighteen statements about human behaviour, based on the imagined proportion of people who'd act in one way or another. Some of the 'statistics' are specific: 'Worthy of empathy: / ninety-nine'. Other insights are presented in rough numbers: 'more than half, for sure'. Still more are contingent – on time, or experience: 'eighty-three, / sooner or later'. Still others 'it's better not to know / not even approximately.'

Wisława Szymborska may be communicating her actual opinions about the human condition, but I find it far more likely that her statements are designed to elicit a response, something like, *That's ridiculous, it's far better/worse than that.* Her statistics are a fabrication, delivered with a confidence that reveals and disguises; revealing what we think in response to her and disguising how beguiling any statistic – real or imagined – can be. It's a tool that elicits a reaction. I heard a ridiculous statistic on the radio this morning, and heard myself talking back to the journalist.

Imagined numbers, giving insight into an imagined control group of one hundred imaginary people. It is this hinge of the known and the strange that holds the work together. Her observations purport to be about behaviour, but they also elicit behaviour from her readers – the poem begs a response, even if it is to question its very premise.

The categories for measurement indicate a curiosity

about people's relationship to time, judgement, selflessness, virtue, admiration, foolishness, group behaviour, fear, contentment, circumstances, relationship to objects or pain. Some of the numbers are modest, and some are generous, and others middling. Those 'who always know better', those 'Unsure of every step' and those 'ready to help / as long as it doesn't take long' propose middling figures, as does 'led to error / by youth'. According to this logic, more than half of us '[turn] savage in crowds . . . for sure'. We all die. All except one are '[w]orthy of empathy' and a significant proportion of us live in 'constant fear / of someone or something'. Few of us, though – only one out of five – are '[c]apable of happiness', roughly the same count as those of us who can 'admire without envy'. A tiny proportion of the population, just three, are just if 'it takes effort to understand.'

Bravery isn't mentioned directly but is present throughout, as is cowardice. Love isn't named, but I feel its absence in 'Doubled over in pain, / without a flashlight in the dark'. Empathy may be a word for love, and Szymborska thinks most of us are 'worthy' of that.

Getting nothing out of life but things:
thirty
(although I would like to be wrong).

Why does this statement elicit such a clear, albeit parenthetical, comment from the speaker? Why would they like to be wrong? The aside – wry and weary and clever – serves as a lament: *don't expect too much from others.* It's also a warning: *don't be surprised at your own motivations.* Does she believe herself? It's hard to know.

Wisława Szymborska is known for an elusive, yet incisive voice – and Joanna Trzeciak Huss's translations maintain the subtle present-yet-absent insights of the poet. Mostly I think she's questioning truth, numbers, categories and opinions about human behaviour. *You never know with people*, a friend of mine said the other day after I'd shared an old grief. At no point in 'A Word on Statistics' is scientific methodology used to arrive at the conclusions. It's a work of art pretending to contain scientific analysis, but it's we readers who become the experiment, as the poem observes our relationship to fact and conduct.

Where do I fall in the numbers presented? In the blank spaces of the page, or the pauses in the breath of recitation, I fill in the gaps with my desire to be perceived as doing better, knowing better, going the extra mile, especially when it takes effort. Rather than question the source or the science, I take the supposed fact for granted and hope I come out well, or well enough. Is this a trap? Or is it a strange door leading into serious conversation?

I used this poem in a class once, and in response to 'Always good, / because they cannot be otherwise: / four – well, maybe five' someone had a point of view I'd not previously considered. I'd always seen 'Always good' as an indication of behaviour, but this group participant – a Black woman in the US – heard 'Always good' as an expectation put upon her. Resilience has been a popular word in the recent decade, and she shared her disdain for the term, saying that resilience praises those who respond to straitened circumstances without critiquing those who create the very circumstances that demand resilience. I loved what happened in this conversation. Wisława Szymborska's words, in brilliant translation, functioned as a mirror for a roomful of people who were grappling with human behaviour. A poem is a living thing, not entirely controllable, and art is made in the space between the work and its reception.

Whatever its veracity, I find this section hard to read without it catching my breath:

Cruel
when forced by circumstances:
it's better not to know
not even approximately.

Why is it 'better not to know'? The statement implies that the speaker knows the number is close to comprehensive. Humanity's virtues are held against our capacity for brutality in a poem that also considers almost all of us 'worthy of empathy'. Wisława Szymborska is appraising herself, perhaps; certainly the 'Statistics' look back to me; but it also is art that reflects on a society. She won the Nobel Prize for Literature in 1996, a Polish woman whose work spanned the latter half of the twentieth century. Does she believe that our worst exploits are worthy of forgiveness? I don't know. I don't believe she's making statements, rather, she's doing what artists do: posing questions.

Is change possible? When I demonstrate the weaker side of some of these statistics, am I capable of change? Art can be a place for self-reflection, and it may be that the poem's desire is to elicit such thoughts. Art is also capable of stating the brutal and uncomfortable truth: many of our avoidant actions are based on the dream of delaying our end. But even then:

Mortal:
one hundred out of one hundred –
a figure that has never varied yet.

Growing up gay during a time when that was unsafe information to share made me a skilled observer of the power dynamics of groups: I always knew the way out; I knew diversion tactics; I knew how to test the waters for acceptance while minimising the risk of hurt. That skill has served me but also failed me: when I allowed others to set the temperature of engagement, I missed out on the possibility of spontaneity, or of being opinionated. Poetry has taught me how to enjoy the spontaneous, to lay aside my worries, to not make resolution a demeaning demand. I have learnt – and am learning still – how to do that in life.

I Invite My Parents to a Dinner Party
Chen Chen

In the invitation, I tell them for the seventeenth time
(the fourth in writing), that I am gay.

In the invitation, I include a picture of my boyfriend
& write, *You've met him two times. But this time,*

you will ask him things other than can you pass the
whatever. You will ask him

about him. You will enjoy dinner. You will be
enjoyable. Please RSVP.

They RSVP. They come.
They sit at the table & ask my boyfriend

the first of the conversation starters I slip them
upon arrival: *How is work going?*

I'm like the kid in *Home Alone*, orchestrating
every movement of a proper family, as if a pair

of scary yet deeply incompetent burglars
is watching from the outside.

My boyfriend responds in his chipper way.
I pass my father a bowl of fish ball soup – *So comforting,*

isn't it? My mother smiles her best
Sitting with Her Son's Boyfriend

Who Is a Boy Smile. I smile my Hurray for Doing
a Little Better Smile.

Everyone eats soup.
Then, my mother turns

to me, whispers in Mandarin, *Is he coming with you
for Thanksgiving? My good friend is & she wouldn't like*

this. I'm like the kid in *Home Alone*, pulling
on the string that makes my cardboard mother

more motherly, except she is
not cardboard, she is

already, exceedingly my mother. Waiting
for my answer.

While my father opens up
a *Boston Globe*, when the invitation

clearly stated: *No security
blankets*. I'm like the kid

in *Home Alone*, except the home
is my apartment, & I'm much older, & not alone,

& not the one who needs
to learn, has to— *Remind me*

what's in that recipe again, my boyfriend says
to my mother, as though they have always, easily

talked. As though no one has told him
many times, what a nonlinear slapstick meets

slasher flick meets psychological
pit he is now co-starring in.

Remind me, he says
to our family.

The first time I read Chen Chen's poem 'I Invite My Parents to a Dinner Party' I knew immediately that I respected the speaker, liked them, and wanted to hear more about what they knew. The voice is skilled, prepared, analytical, detached, mostly patient, caring, hopeful, realistic, artistic and even open to surprise. What's not to like?

The best predictor of the future is the past, the old adage goes. That may or may not be true, but it's a powerful idea nonetheless. Patterns – even good ones – once established, are often difficult to break out of, and in these unfurling couplets, the speaker is working hard to disrupt a family pattern. This is neither the first nor the second time the parents have met their son's boyfriend – *'you've met him two times. But this time, // you will . . .'* – but there yet remains a hope that the third encounter may be the opportunity for the predictable behaviour of the parents' patterns to change. There is understanding offered – the parents need security blankets, and are concerned about how others will speak about them – but their determined offspring is calling forth a deeper ethic of courtesy and kindness.

The son, for his part, also gives us much information about himself: he is persistent –'the seventeenth time / (the fourth in writing)' – and prepared – 'I include a picture' – and assertive – *'You will ask him // about him. You will enjoy dinner. You will be / enjoyable. Please RSVP.'* He knows – or, at least, he thinks he knows – his parents and their foibles, and has prepared conversation starters which he 'slip[s] them / upon arrival'. The son bears the responsibility for educating his parents in how to be hospitable to his partner, and while he knows they are likely to disappoint him he's open to accepting even minor improvements: 'I smile my Hurray for Doing / a Little Better Smile.'

The son's predictive capacities are many: he anticipates fears, he has strategies for responding to resistance and even indifference, he facilitates the encounter even in the midst of modest expectations. Where there are limitations, he attempts to provide practical opportunities, and he navigates linguistic, cultural and emotional gulfs. It isn't only charm that he utilises, he also is persuasive, beguiling and guiding. He's got a timeframe in mind: he's not expecting radical change, just gradual improvement. And as far as he's able, he's moderating his anger – although the hurt that underlies most anger is clear in the poem, particularly in the references to *Home Alone*. Finally, he gives incentives: the promise of the final two words: *our* and *family*, which is another way of saying that deeper love is the natural outcome of such effort.

There's something else: exhaustion and responsibility, which he wishes wasn't his to bear. Why is it that the son bears this burden of responsibility? It's clear he believes his parents are – or could be – 'enjoyable'. They've not met the mark of cordiality in previous encounters but he's hoping they'll make progress: '*this time, // you will ask him things other than can you pass the / whatever*'. He wants the boyfriend to be seen, appreciated as a person, not just as another body at a dinner table, someone to be tolerated. He wants to be seen too, as a son – a gay son – with a romantic life, with a home to which he invites his parents, with parents he can be proud of, whose affection is evident and even shared. In short, he believes in change; or is willing to suspend his belief in the possibility of possibility. He's also desperate – understandably – as one who is trying to make the unlikely a little less unlikely. He's 'like the kid in *Home Alone*, pulling / on the string that makes my cardboard mother // more motherly'.

The parents come across as social: they have friends who come for Thanksgiving. But they are also anxious about what the neighbours might think. Would the parents recognise themselves in the anxieties of their son? Even if they wouldn't recognise themselves, is the speaking voice accurate? Any particular experience of conflict can elicit curiosity about the other point of view, whether that point of view is to our liking or not. Information is contained even in misperception.

One of the themes explored is the great gulf between people who use different social languages. One language is saying: please value what's important in my life; please show me that you love all of me, not just part of me; please be the enjoyable people that I know you can be; please talk. Beneath Chen Chen's humour is a plea, a word etymologically linked to pleasing, yes, but also linked to wrangle, determine and litigate. The speaker – skilled in observing, analysing, preparing – is filled with yearning: for affirmation, for some tolerable level of encounter and resolve. And the language spoken by the parents? We don't know much: they come to dinner, certainly. They also accept – and attempt to fulfill, at least initially – his instructions on how to do a little better. They seem unsure of how to speak this new language, though, and are in need of some comfort. How strange, how true, how difficult that those whose assurance, affirmation and affection is yearned for are themselves in need of assurance, affirmation and affection. The same hunger seems to run through parents and son, each finding the other a little bewildering, each bonded to the other, each separated from the other. What will bridge them, beyond the gestures that they are trying – succeeding, failing, pleading, flailing – to make around this dinner table?

Chen Chen's depiction of the boyfriend's character is deft. His direct speech is an interruption: the son amidst his many desires is seeking control, but then the boyfriend interrupts the internal monologue of his burdened lover. '*Remind me*' he says. There are three people around a table who share history, too much of it, it seems. Yet the boyfriend, a relative newcomer, is able to invent a past that contains conversations about a recipe. His burdens are not the burdens of the son and parents. His imaginative creativity sparks the ground for a new encounter. In a way, he is the energy of a poem. He interrupts and his interruption resets, makes a new vista unfold before them. The long sentences, spread across couplets of varying line length, may be begging for a different form, just as the lines of communication between a son and his parents is also in need of a new shape.

The groundwork – the meal, the invitation, the instructions, the guidance – led to this. Without the son's preparations, the fresh moment of the boyfriend's generosity wouldn't have had the opportunity to arise. But the speaker's anxieties about his parents limit his own spontaneity. It was the openness to the moment that was needed, what Tolkien called the *eucatastraophe*: the resolution of a catastrophe into a success. The success is contingent on the possibility of failure, and the belief – as hidden, as distant as it may be – that failure can be interrupted by what hitherto seemed unimaginable.

For a long time I worked with Corrymeela, a peace and reconciliation community whose main centre is located on the north coast of Ireland. Corrymeela's been there since 1965, and, in fact, the organisation gets its name from the land: the fields on which the main house is built were called Corrymeelagh, a name that is uncertain in its meaning.

The buildings on that site have come and gone, having hosted thousands of dialogues, retreats and meetings. The buildings are not what's sacred about that site, it's the views that are important. Every meeting room has windows looking out to the sea: that narrow strait between the north-east coast of Ireland and the west coast of Britain: deep waters, beautiful, full of both visible and hidden tides. That view is the companion to dialogues about peace and conflict and violence and resolution. It is a present partner, drawing the ear and eye, drawing the water in our bodies too.

from **Conflict Resolution for Holy Beings**
Joy Harjo

> *I am the holy being of my mother's prayer and my father's song.*

NORMAN PATRICK BROWN,

DINEH POET AND SPEAKER

I. SET CONFLICT RESOLUTION GROUND RULES:

Recognize whose lands these are on which we stand.
Ask the deer, turtle, and the crane.
Make sure the spirits of these lands are respected and
   treated with goodwill.
The land is a being who remembers everything.
You will have to answer to your children, and their children,
   and theirs –
The red shimmer of remembering will compel you up the
   night to walk the perimeter of truth for understanding.
As I brushed my hair over the hotel sink to get ready I
   heard:
By listening we will understand who we are in this holy
   realm of words.
Do not parade, pleased with yourself.
You must speak in the language of justice.

When I trained in conflict mediation, we used the metaphor of the spine – that extraordinary column of thirty-three interlocking vertebrae, attached to nerves and muscles – as the shape for resolution practice. The spine is fixed for strength yet flexible enough for movement and modification. The idea was that if you had a *spine* of conflict resolution practices then you could work intuitively with groups using that structure, flexing it, amending it, utilising it.

The conflict mediation model I learnt was typical: firstly, it asserts that conflict is made up of interlocking relationships, issues, behaviour and feelings. We were taught the art of an initial assessment with parties to the conflict before a facilitated exchange in a trustable environment, based on which some agreement about the important issues is built. Typically, we'd address a relatively straightforward area of disagreement in the first instance, to gain momentum and deepen confidence for discussing trickier problems. Of course, there's no straightforward pathway through interpersonal tensions, and even seemingly simple conflicts can have umbilical connections to profoundly complex ones: I might be upset with someone because of how they behaved last week; they might be disempowered because of my behaviour over a decade.

When I came across Joy Harjo's book *Conflict Resolution for Holy Beings*, I was intrigued. I was on holiday in Seattle, with a lot of time for reading, so I bought it, took it back to my room, and read it in a single sitting. The next day, I read it again. The title poem takes a six-part conflict-resolution framework and writes a response to each:

1. SET CONFLICT RESOLUTION GROUND RULES
2. USE EFFECTIVE COMMUNICATION SKILLS THAT DISPLAY AND ENHANCE MUTUAL TRUST AND RESPECT
3. GIVE CONSTRUCTIVE FEEDBACK
4. REDUCE DEFENSIVENESS AND BREAK THE DEFENSIVENESS CHAIN
5. ELIMINATE NEGATIVE ATTITUDES DURING CONFLICT
6. AND, USE WHAT YOU LEARN TO RESOLVE YOUR OWN CONFLICTS AND TO MEDIATE OTHERS' CONFLICTS

Before looking at the first section, it's useful to consider the whole framework. It is a model that addresses the particulars of a conflict, as well as the emotions that result when addressing it – resolution sometimes heightens conflict before transforming or reducing it. Joy Harjo's model is interested in the ecosystem of relationships, the chain of defensiveness that can affect others, or repeat its patterns in the future.

'Ground rules' is a phrase that's used often, in classrooms, in workplaces, in interviews. Some people speak about setting up a contract before a group embarks on a dialogue process. Some eschew legal language in favour of nature-based language, and others return to legal language having found more artistic language unhelpful. Ground rules, at their best, help to establish a framework for addressing interpersonal communication. Joy Harjo's usage of 'ground rules' reframes this. She focuses on the setting, the earth upon which all relationships occur. She centres and deepens the question of locale: 'The land is a being who remembers everything.' Land is an interested and affected party in all our histories: a party with a voice, agency, insight, intelligence. Land has precedence in this first of six parts: land's lifespan is vast.

Harjo questions ownership – thereby power – stating that other living beings need to be considered and consulted: 'the deer, turtle, and the crane'.

While Joy Harjo favours the 'ground' in 'ground rules', the first section of her six-part poem is not lacking in firm instruction – an observation of the imperative verbs reveals that: set, recognise, ask, make sure, you will have to answer, compel, walk, do not parade, you must speak. This is a poem with a profound moral agenda, a poem that does not shy away from tasking humanity with a cause: 'walk the perimeter of truth for understanding'. Here, art is given a clear role: to be the vehicle that communicates a message. I'm always moved by the modification from instruction to narrative. It is as if Harjo is attributing the words to a source beyond her so that when she shows up in the poem – 'As I brushed my hair over the hotel sink' – she's also a listener. She, possibly with a mirror in front of her, is examining herself: the rules are for all and the conduit is no exception. The rulemaker is no human authority.

With 'Make sure the spirits of these lands are respected and treated with goodwill', Harjo links that treatment with the history of what has occurred in a place, what is buried in the land, what might grow, what might reoccur, what might lie hidden. It's as if the poet is saying everything is in everything: the conflict that needed to be resolved today is linked to us, to the land, to the past, to the dead, to the

31

spiritual life, and to what's to come. Harjo's poem is a call to action, community and courage. Conflict is part of the human experience, a part of being *Holy Beings*. The tree, the land, the turtle, the panther, the puma, the deer, the woman brushing her hair in the sink . . . all holy beings. Being present to our bodies will aid our pilgrimage and resolution:

The red shimmer of remembering will compel you up the night to walk the perimeter of truth for understanding.

It is by walking *around*, and not *through* truth that we will discover what it is that holds us in its perimeter.

We negotiate ordinary conflicts often: everyday non-abusive conflict is one of the electricities of life, or it has the potential to be. We experience this energy in our relationships, and also in our own internal world. How do we live with, and learn from these conflicts? In ever-improving ways, we hope. Most of us have conflict resolution systems; sometimes defined, sometimes not. You might have one particular approach with a child, another with a sibling, and yet another with a friend. You might be fluent in a resolution style in friendships yet feel unsure how to act in a new workplace. You might have found yourself derailed when conflict evokes old baggage. You may find that your conflict style suits some, but not others, thereby inviting you to develop multiple approaches. The task is to see what works well – or well enough – in given situations.

We humans are but one part of what occurs on the earth; we are just one among many body-bound breathing beings; subject to conflicts within or outside of our control; affected by old wounds yet seeking change. The wisdom of Joy Harjo's poem is in its groundedness. It doesn't look to land simply as a *metaphor* for resolution, but rather recognises the ground as an active participant. It expands engagement, and by doing so, positions us humans as just one participant among all the *Holy Beings*.

This morning I read some of Camus's *The Myth of Sisyphus*, about a man condemned to push a big stone up a hill for eternity. As soon as he nears the crest of a hill, he's overpowered by the size of the stone, and it rolls back down. Him too. He starts again.

I've been finding myself in a rut of thinking lately: unhelpful patterns that are difficult to break. I wanted to know what'd help. I talk to friends. I read psychoanalysis. (Hell, I even pay for some.) The reading helped this morning. I saw things in Sisyphus that I didn't want to see. I saw things in me too.

Eurydice, Turning

Rita Dove

Each evening I call home and my brother answers.
Each evening my rote patter, his unfailing cheer –
until he swivels; leans in, louder:

'It's your daughter, Mom! Want to say
hello to Rita?' My surprise each time
that he still asks, believes in asking.

'Hello, Rita.' A good day, then;
the voice as fresh as I remember.
I close my eyes to savor it

but don't need the dark to see her
younger than my daughter now,
wasp-waisted in her home-sewn coral satin

with all of Bebop yet to boogie through.
No wonder Orpheus, when he heard
the voice he'd played his lyre for

in the only season of his life that mattered,
could not believe she was anything
but who she'd always been to him, for him . . .

Silence, open air. I know what's coming,
wait for my brother's 'OK, now say
goodbye, Mom' – and her parroted reply:

'Goodbye, Mom.'
That lucid, ghastly singing.
I put myself back into a trance

and keep talking: weather, gossip, news.

I saw a family photo of old friends the other day: grandparents; their daughter and her partner; their grandchildren. The photo was taken on a bright and blustery November day in Scotland. They looked fresh from a chilly wind. I guess some had tears in their eyes from the cold. I licked my lips looking at the photo, imagining the salt in the air. Molly, the grandmother, whom I know well, looked especially happy. Beaming. Next to her, her husband, also a friend, smiled in a tired way. Same with the daughter. Molly is in the early stages of dementia. As these things go, it's not the worst case. Forgetting who she is, where she is, and – bit by bit – forgetting other people. She loves the bright walks, I hear. She loves to cuddle the youngest.

When I got a new job in my late twenties, Molly phoned and said 'let's go for whiskey.' She knew everybody in my new workplace and was filled with delicious gossip, insight, and story. She gave good advice, bought me a second whiskey, and also chatted about her life. I like her company immensely. And there she is, in the photo, present and smiling and wind-woken and fading. No wonder the others look a little tired. They needed the winter air too. Bracing: for themselves and the new shape of love they'll have to bear.

Rita Dove's poem 'Eurydice, Turning' is about such bracing. A woman calls her brother every evening and a pattern unfolds: the brother answers with his 'unfailing cheer' and then, speaking a little louder, he passes the phone to their mother, with a deft and well-practiced 'It's your daughter, Mom! Want to say / hello to Rita?' Easy language but filled with information and reminders. He's helping their mother remember who she is, that she has a daughter, that her daughter's name is Rita, that the purpose in passing the phone to her is so that the mother can say hello. The mother does as much as she's told, and perhaps as much as she's capable of: 'Hello, Rita.'

In two words, the poet – and Rita's name is echoed twice in this poem, like a signature, like a reminder to herself of who she is – understands that it is a good day. What makes it so? The absence of refusal, or confusion, the simple acquiescence. Ease is measured in such small increments. The voice, too 'as fresh as I remember.' 'Eurydice, Turning' both praises and laments memory – its gifts and its losses. A poet remembers her mother's fading memory. She's the in-between generation: mother to her own daughter, and – for a while – mother to her mother. Memory is physical: she recalls her mother's body and style and skill, 'wasp-waisted in her home-sewn coral satin'; her mother's presence to the future with 'all of Bebop yet to boogie through.' Then, her mother knew the music, the moves to the music, the jazz and improvisation. Now, the contrast: the steps are delivered carefully. 'Want to say / hello to Rita?'

The poem turns: from the scene in which people are separated by memory to a scene from Greek mythology. Orpheus and Eurydice were lovers, but Eurydice died from a serpent bite as she fled an aggressor. Orpheus, a heartbroken musician, descended into the underworld to rescue her, charming all the guardians of the dead with his song. After he found her, they were granted permission to leave on condition that

39

Orpheus walk ahead of Eurydice and not turn back until they were both in sunlight. They came tantalisingly close, but Orpheus, unable to resist, turned too early while she was still in shade, and she faded in front of him. Orpheus not only lost his lover, but also lost himself. He appears like a shade of himself in subsequent myths: forever changed by what he could not hold on to.

Rita Dove turns to this myth as she thinks of everything her mother's voice summons up for her. The Orpheus of her poem is charmed, not by his own music, but by the voice of the one he'd played music for 'in the only season of his life that mattered'. Meaning becomes hollow for the bereft, and it becomes hard to experience what's happening right in front of you: whether you're a storied lover who turned too early, or a poet whose mother's voice is like a ghost of herself.

Why 'Eurydice, Turning' then? Why not 'Orpheus, Turning'? The myth blames Orpheus – with a mixture of love, enthusiasm and poor timing – for turning toward Eurydice before she was fully in sunlight. But Rita Dove has Eurydice turning. Something compelled Eurydice to turn: fate, perhaps, or time. Nothing to be done. Orpheus is not held responsible, he's just left with 'Silence, open air.' The music of memory – Bebop – turns to 'lucid, ghastly singing.'

The characters – Rita, her brother, the mother, Orpheus – are depicted with sensitivity, love and pathos. Families living with a loved one with memory loss carry multi-layered burdens: their own grief; the tensions that arise between siblings about matters to do with care and decision-making; the loneliness of being the child of someone who may not remember whose child you are; the role reversal of parenting a parent. In 'Eurydice, Turning' the absence is both bitter and sweet: bitter because of what's fading away; sweet because between sister and brother, there is tenderness and care and an absence of hostility. The brother is the epitome of patience, reminding his mother who she's speaking to and what is being asked of her; he doesn't demand much, and helps her end the conversation:

'OK, now say
goodbye, Mom' . . .
'Goodbye, Mom.'

These nine stanzas are a masterclass in coping with grief. The daughter does an unbearable thing: to notice what is slowly disappearing. 'I put myself back into a trance', Rita Dove writes, and no small wonder. To be in a trance is to have your eyes fixed on something there, but not quite there. Ordinary exchanges – 'weather, gossip, news' – become a small relief, an automatic reflex, a way to fill the void with language that's easy, unmemorable, a simple carrier of connection, affection and care.

There are three two-word sentences in the poem, and in each, the two words are punctuated with a comma: the title 'Eurydice, Turning'; then 'Hello, Rita'; and finally, 'Goodbye, Mom.' These short end-stopped lines ring the heart. Mythology, and then the voice of the mother, both real and fading: parroting the greeting, fumbling the farewell. The speaker is in conversation with a mother who is intimately known, and infinitely elsewhere. Present and absent. The poet is the bearer of this sadness, this memory, this faith-fulness to the past that is fading for her mother. 'Ghastly' – from Old English gæstan, related to ghost, and aghast – describes something ungraspably present: something to feel, then let go of. In the presence of this strong feeling, there is the absence of either tension or anger between the siblings. Who'd blame a person for losing their mind? Nobody. But it's easy to feel anger in the face of such sadness. Using a myth whose original telling blames one character for not holding on to the other, 'Eurydice, Turning' removes blame and allows us to be present for the extended, exhausting moment of letting go.

While I was writing this, a friend called. Earlier this morning, I'd texted him and mentioned something disappointing that had happened to me yesterday. When my friend got the message, he phoned, and instead of a greeting he said, 'That's shit, man'. He was walking his dog at the time, I could hear the traffic of Belfast, and every now and then he'd pause the conversation to call his pup back. He gave no solution to the disappointment; there wasn't one. He was a voice. Five minutes. He told me a story about work, we made each other laugh, we made plans to meet up when I'm home. For most of the last fifteen years we've lived in different countries; on different continents even. These days I'm in Ireland half the year, so I see him often then. Sometimes, though, I chat more to him when I'm away: phones are blamed for much, but I love the ease of connection.

Ode to My Homegirls
Safia Elhillo

smelling of orange rind   of cardamom
   most beautiful girls in the world   *wake up bitch*
     we're getting waffles   you can keep crying

but you're going out   my marriages
   my alibis   my bright & hardy stalks
     of protea   & all i know of love i learned

at thirteen   dialing basma's home phone
   by heart   to three-way call whatever boy
     so that weeks later   when the phone bill came

only basma's familiar number beside the time stamp
   clearing my name   basma herself staying awake
     for hours   to hang up the phone after

you who send pictures of your rashes
   to the group text   & long voice notes
     from the bathtub   your laughter echoing against the tiles

you who scatter the world's map   piling into
   cheap buses & budget airlines   four of us asleep
     in my dorm bed   six of us overflowing

my studio apartment   false lashes for weeks after
   like commas in my every pillowcase   you clog my toilet
     & admit it   you text me screenshots

from the gucci fashion show   *getting rich*
   so i can get u this   & when i lived alone
      & that man followed me

one night home from the six train
   up lexington   & into the hallway
      tried for hours to break open my front door

you took turns from all your cities   & stayed
   overnight with me on the phone   for three days
      snoring & murmuring in your sleep

How does Safia Elhillo praise friendship? Through the senses: scent – 'smelling of orange rind   of cardamom'; taste – *'wake up bitch / we're getting waffles'*; sound – 'dialing basma's home phone / by heart'; sight – 'pictures of your rashes / to the group text'; and touch – 'four of us asleep / in my dorm bed'.

This ode may even have been written in response to such a prompt. Or perhaps she decided to praise the physicality of friendship by evoking sensory memories. Whatever the source of this poem's structure, it's held together in ten tercets, with each three-line stanza containing a caesura, a place where the line is   cut. There are many reasons why a poet uses such a pause, or rest, mid-line. It can act like a visual breath, or Elhillo may wish to represent the space between friends who are near and also apart. Maybe the pause visualises the lovingly interrupted half-sentences that happen when crowds of friends engage in enlivened conversation.

Elhillo locates the poem at the in-between spaces between friends: their conversations and visits throughout decades of their lives. The teenage phone calls where one friend is the conduit for another to talk with 'whatever boy'. Basma's 'familiar' number is known 'by heart'. As friendships and phones develop, their mobiles carry pictures of each other's bodies and are the means by which plans for 'cheap buses & budget airlines' are communicated. They hear each other from the bath, 'your laughter echoing against the tiles.' These are friends who have survived difficulties and who have found freedom, protection, delight, disclosure and home in the community of each other; 'Homegirls' means everything it can possibly mean in this hymn of love. Girls from home; girls who are each other's home.

Sometimes, when feeling my way through a poem, I read it out loud (by myself – I don't want too many stares) and listen to the intuitive volume that the work brings out in me. The opening energy of 'Ode to My Homegirls' is bright, vivacious – the joy is impossible to avoid. By the end, the tone has changed and, I, too, am quietened: short sentences whispered on the phone through the night. *Girls That Never Die* is the title of the book in which this ode is published; a book replete with stories of change, love, Muslim experiences of America, power, language and delight.

I am living in New York as I write this, so I can visualise 'the six train', the subway that shoots up the east side of Manhattan with many stops along Lexington Avenue, situated between Third and Fourth Avenues. I was on it yesterday, knowing I'd write about 'Ode to My Homegirls' this morning. I realised I was looking at everyone, wondering who they'll text for a laugh, or for a listening ear, or for companionship. I looked around hoping that nobody would be followed 'into the hallway' by a man who'd try 'for hours to break open my front door.' This ode led me to consider the poem evoked in the text messages sent by passengers on the train, and all the destinations of those messages: 'you took turns from all your cities'. As the ode ends, it has moved into sound beyond language: friends so close they leave their phones on all night, so as to hear each other 'snoring & murmuring in your sleep'.

A few years ago, I realised that I wanted to be better at keeping in touch with friends, not only catching up when circumstance affords it, or responding when someone messages me. While I have an inner resistance to systems, I nonetheless made a simple list of people to contact every month. When I'm awake in the middle of the night I message a friend. A simple hello. They're often up (timezones or insomnia or both) and I hear what's happening. Perhaps not the big story, but often the little one: something funny, something strange, something familiar. Despite my resistance to lists, I'm glad for this one.

Distance is not a barrier to Safia Elhillo. Another way to understand the caesura could be as a visual demonstration of connection: countries, miles, days, nights, threats, sleep. 'Ode to My Homegirls' praises the phone that bridges separation: *'getting rich / so i can get u this'*. Such a text is a *wish you were here* perhaps, or – even deeper – it's a *you are here with me, and I know you so well, I know what you like to wear, and I'd get it for you if I could*. Each layer of casual communication is a container for a message of loyalty and love: 'my bright & hardy stalks / of protea' – a flower both beautiful and strong, known for surviving drought, rain and fire. The phone signifies communication, and communication signifies connection. Connection, further, points to commitment, which points to . . . what? Love is the obvious answer: the kind of love that is demonstrated by decades, fun, memories, confession of clogged toilets, and travel; the kind of love that stays awake at night providing breath and sound, and everything contained in breath and sound: safety, proximity, home.

For years I was frightened of anger, which, no surprise, made my anger all the more potent. I tried forcing myself into reconciliation, but that was fuelled more by fear than healing.

Poetry helped: I wrote rhymes and lines to capture and change my point of view. Sometimes I wondered what the point was: a poem wasn't moving me onwards. Something happened, though, when I saw my rage on the page: I could look at it. And, little by little, it looked back, and revealed other layers to me.

What he should have had

Sasha taqʷšəblu LaPointe

It's not fair says my
brother talking at me over
his pint glass

I belong on a yacht we
had that you know we
had a yacht

we never had a yacht
you mean one of mom's boyfriends did I poke
at the red-filmed ice of my spent Bloody Mary
I order another as my brother continues his story
of what we should have had

all that shit he
says *those rich*
guys those condos
 in the city

but she moved us to
Swinomish

at this there is a long sigh an
eye roll another beer in his
fist and he drinks it angrily

and I am noticing
how handsome my
brother is

his pitch-colored hair his jaw
his big smile how he looks
like Superman like Freddie
Prinze Jr. in some romantic
comedy made for teenagers
in the nineties

driving back up the coast to
our ancestral home I sleep in
the woods send him pictures of
whales and a roadside motel
we stayed in as kids

but he is busy with his
list of all the things we
should have had

he is writing them down
and marking them off

when we say goodbye I
watch my older brother try
not to cry

I tell him to be less
angry

but it's too late my brother has
already pulled out his boning
knife

look what happened to you

he repeats it

he carves a fish shaped hole
right into me

look what happened to you

People who've grown up with each other share a language so profound even their arguments are intimate. Sasha taqʷšəblu LaPointe's poem 'What he should have had' articulates this language in its direct speech, linebreaks and blank space.

These characters know each other: they're sharing drinks, and are able to lament as well as challenge each other. '[W]e / had a yacht' has an equal but opposite, 'you mean one of mom's boyfriends'. This is a relationship where siblings know they can 'poke', even while one is in a certain amount of despair. They differ enormously in temperament, and the impression gained through these short lines is that distance is growing, not being bridged. Despite that, the sister still texts him pictures and memories.

Each character represents a response to pain. In a way, they are depicted as binary opposites: he's angry and she 'tell[s] him to be less / angry'. But the linebreak between 'less' and 'angry' gives a hint about point of view: the brother feels like he's being told 'to be less'.

Despite the itinerant nature of their childhood, her point of view is settled: sleeping in the woods, she sends 'pictures of / whales' and recalls memories of a motel. He, however, has lists and a 'boning / knife'. '[L]ook what happened to you' he says, and then the line is repeated, without italics: 'look what happened to you'. The siblings belong to each other, linked by wounds, and also by a widening chasm.

What did happen? I'm not sure, but in the unfolding lines, I hear how history and choices and pain have led them in different directions. 'Look', the speaker pleads, perhaps asking her brother to give attention to his sorrow, the kind of attention that may help, or heal. 'Look', the brother replies later on in the poem, and repeats this imperative too. He has something else in his sights.

The brother feels like he should have had more, that things are not fair. He's having some drinks with his sister, and recounting 'his story / of what we should have had'. Anger is often a story with many layers, so I wonder what the brother's anger is about. It finds a focus in their mother, the 'she' who moved them to Swinomish, away from *those rich / guys*' and their '*condos / in the city*'. It could also be about a whole host of understandable things: disentitlements, the discrimination toward the Indigenous Coast Salish nation the siblings are members of, opportunity denied.

I feel the brother's outrage, and the impact of it. And also, through the point of view of the narrator, worry that his outrage is hurting himself. Perhaps the poet is annoyed that her brother is caught up in cycles of anger that wound him; maybe the brother is annoyed that his sister has settled for a compromise too far. She seems contained; he seems uncontained. He shares his pain when he 'carves a fish shaped hole / right into me'. What is this? A door through which something can come in or out? An opening for pain, a wound? A different connection with the past? A connection between them both? The pain felt where a brother disappeared? The bond is strained and intimate. The root-deep differences between them are, presumably, hard won.

Anger is a powerful experience: it can be a mechanism to control others or something you feel controlled by; it can be a release of emotion; it can be an attempt to shut down other emotions; it can cover or it can expose. Anger is a site of policing: some people automatically see anger as something to quell, others see it as a necessary expression. While some use anger as an excuse to justify aggression, others see it as part of a creative artistic process. Anger takes different shapes in different cultures and comes with rules and hierarchies, and consequences or promises. Depending on your age and gender, anger can be interpreted in different ways: some people are rewarded for expressing anger; others are punished for it.

It can be hard to pay attention when angry. Depending on the person, anger may want something else before what lies beneath it can be explored: some roar of energy, something physical, some exercising release, some reparation, some apology. All reasonable. Anger may need permission, too: some people have grown up with their strong emotions being surveilled, or judged. It may want something outside of the individual: somebody may not be satisfied with dealing with their own anger while the larger, more systemic issues that caused the injury continue: injustices, oversights, consequences that stretch through time. Anger can be an appeal for restorative attention: the decisions that affected your life; the life that's been predisposed never to have a yacht, a condo '*all that shit*'.

It's too easy to imagine that the anger in 'What he should have had' is explained by alcohol. After all, they're both drinking: he's on beers, she's on Bloody Marys. It's entirely possible that one or the other felt like the alcohol eased their nerves. It's also entirely possible that alcohol covered or quelled the creative energy underneath anger. The alcohol could also have been a scene of hospitality: siblings sharing time. The trajectory of the poem – pain, discussion, drinks, differing versions of history, separation – is all too familiar to many of us. Reading the lines, I find myself reading myself, thinking of when I've been angry, or when I've hoped someone I love could arrive at a point of view that damages them less.

Facing the brother's distress is a sister who *sees* him: his pain, but also his body, his handsomeness:

> his pitch-colored hair his jaw
> his big smile how he looks
> like Superman like Freddie
> Prinze Jr. in some romantic
> comedy made for teenagers
> in the nineties

I feel a plea here: for the brother to see himself through the lens that the sister does. That somehow, in all the valid rage resulting from pain, he could find pathways that help. But the speaker knows that nobody can do the work of change for another. Together in friendship or family, we are also alone: and the inner work of reconciliation cannot be forced.

Poetry is a lonely business, and in 'What he should have had' I see the wisdom gained through this loneliness. The sister who wishes a brother to be grounded in his own body knows she cannot decide this for him. She, however, maintains and contains herself, she makes body memories of her own, forging belonging through writing, art, memories, land – 'I sleep in / the woods'.

Last summer I sat on a train, looking out the window. (I always feel short-changed if I'm in a train seat without a view.) As we crossed a viaduct, a bird of prey – I don't know what it was, a peregrine? – casually glided alongside the carriage, just a few feet from the window. It was matching our speed: quick for us, seemingly easy for the raptor. I could see the sunlight on its edges. Somehow – I don't know how – it tilted its mesmeric, dangerous body then swooped down, in a fall of precision and beauty.

I've thought about that bird all year. Its claws, its hunger, its skill. The way it moved through the air, the way I could – for an instant – see from the same vantage point.

Someday I Will Visit Hawk Mountain

M. Soledad Caballero

I will be a real birder and know raptors
by the shape of their wings, the span of them
against wide skies, the browns and grays
of their feathers, the reds and whites like specks
of paint. I will look directly into the sun, point and say,
those are black vultures, those are red-shouldered
hawks. They fly with the thermals, updrafts, barely
moving, glide their bodies along the currents, borrowing
speed from the wind. I will know other raptors,
sharp-shinned hawk, the Cooper's hawk, the ones
that flap their wings and move their bodies during the day.
The merlins, the peregrine falcons, soaring like bullets
through blue steel, cutting the winds looking for rabbits,
groundhogs that will not live past talons and claws.
I will know the size of their bones, the weight
of their beaks. I will remember the curves, the colors
of their oval, yellow eyes. I will have the measurements,
the data that live inside their bodies like a secret
taunting me to find its guts. Or this is what I tell myself.
But, I am a bad birder. I care little about the exact rate
of a northern goshawk's flight speed. I do not need
to know how many pounds of food an American kestrel
eats in winter. I have no interest in the feather types
on a turkey vulture. I have looked up and forgotten
these facts again and again and again. They float
out of my mind immediately. What I remember:
my breathless body as I look into the wildness above,
raptors flying, diving, stooping, bodies of light, talismans,
incantations, dust of the gods. Creatures of myth,

they hang in the sky like questions. They promise
nothing, indifferent to everything but death.
Still, still, I catch myself gasping, neck craned up,
follow the circles they build out of sky, reach
for their brutal mystery, the alien spark of more.

'I will be a real birder and know . . .' M. Soledad Caballero begins. A *real* birder, as opposed to what? An unreal one? 'Someday I Will Visit Hawk Mountain' opens, then, with a kind of tension: somebody loves something but isn't sure if they're entitled to love it because they feel like they're an amateur, a dabbler, a fledgling perhaps. Even the destination – Hawk Mountain; a bird sanctuary in Pennsylvania USA with a particular interest in birds of prey – contains a mild level of tension: she hasn't been yet, but '[s]omeday'.

What would a real birder be? Someone who knows? And what would they know? How to identify a particular kind of bird by the shape and span of its wings, the flecks on their feathers, the patterns of their flights, their interaction with the wind, their nocturnal habits, prey, weight, beak-shape and eye colour? This exact knowledge is praised by a speaker who – ironically – tells the reader details of what she does not know; all the while demonstrating a familiarity with the particulars of different raptors. For someone who isn't – according to themselves anyway – a 'real' birder, they know a lot about what they do not know. 'But, I am a bad birder' appears as a turn a little over halfway through the poem's block of a single-stanza body. If a real birder were to be typified by knowing, a bad birder is described by what details she does not care about: 'I care little about the exact . . .' she declares, detailing more information: flight speed, eating habits and feather type. 'I have looked up and forgotten / these facts again and again and again.' This is someone who cared enough to look up – as information in a book, or online, yes, but the first meaning of 'look up' receives more attention: the physical act of looking up seems to captivate the poet to such a level that data becomes secondary. Facts 'float / out of my mind immediately' in the face of such wonderment:

raptors flying, diving, stooping, bodies of light, talismans, incantations, dust of the gods. Creatures of myth . . .

It seems Caballero is exploring the relationship between information and observation. Would it aid her watching? Would it deepen her wonder? Would knowledge act as an impediment to the existential questions that birds pose? To know their aeronautical proportions or eating habits would, perhaps, imply that the flying creature is understood through the conduit of such information. Instead, information floats away, and something else occurs: the poet's voice rises to orchestral rapture in the face of such beauty: wild, 'indifferent', 'brutal' and 'alien'. Lacking in the poem – a deliberate absence – are anthropomorphic projections onto the raptors, as well as any prescriptions that see birds as a metaphor for meaning. They may 'hang in the sky like questions' but they're also 'indifferent to everything but death.' Seeing them is not a prescription for escapism, it's a recognition of the world; a world of transcendence or thrill as well as talons.

I don't see 'Someday I Will Visit Hawk Mountain' as dismissive about scientific information, rather I read it as asking critical questions about the relationship between knowledge and wonder. There is no shortage of learning – from experts, friends, books, old stories – in the work.

Expertise is evidenced and praised. But knowledge is not seen as the only lens through which to experience what unfolds in the spectacle of observation.

Birds are named, in both classification and particularity: raptors, black vultures, red-shouldered hawks, sharp-shinned hawk, Cooper's hawk, merlins, peregrine falcons, northern goshawk, American kestrel, turkey vulture. Their features too: wingspan, feather colour, flying patterns, speed, the fate of the rabbits and groundhogs who will not survive the birds' 'talons and claws'. Also curves and colours, all the 'measurements, / the data that live inside their bodies like a secret / taunting me to find its guts'. Every time I read it, I find myself wondering if the 'guts' of the secret is also a critique of a predatory imagination that may be inherent in some forms of knowing: to comprehend certain features of a creature is not to know it inside out: there will always be the unknown.

Information, then, is a precursor, and as the poem reaches its own culmination, it soars – through language – in response to the poet's memory and experience. No species or particular scientific classification or description is given in the final lines. Instead: 'Still, still' – the irony continues, to be still in the face of such movement. Even time stops in the face of creatures in time and instead of the birds being captured, 'I catch myself'. Knowledge's desire is superseded by experience's devotion: 'gasping, neck craned up, / follow the circles they build out of sky, reach . . .' Bird classifications aren't the only thing to fade; the speaker's 'I will' fades too: initially it's repeated six times, from the title to the opening line 'I will be a real birder' then 'I will look directly into the sun' and 'I will know other raptors,' 'I will know the size of their bones,' 'I will remember the curves' and 'I will have the measurements.' These declarations of will are statements of intention and achievement. The verbs of intention change, though, and move toward relinquishment: This is what I tell myself . . . I am a bad birder. I care little about . . . I do not need . . . I have no interest. Ambition gives way to experience: 'What I remember . . . as I look'. 'More' is the final word. More what? I'm guessing there will be more knowledge to accompany the abundance already exhibited. But 'the alien spark of more' of the poem's end belongs to the birds, or whatever it is the birds point to – the myths and questions they evoke. If Rainer Maria Rilke looked to God and asked himself the question of the self in the face of that great unknown, Caballero looks to birds and asks the question of existence. A knowledge-seeking creature looks at creatures who hold instinct and knowledge in their magnificent patterns of flight and survival. Subject to hungers and death they may be – poet and raptor – but they are alien to each other. The poet wants more of the unknowing, it seems to me, more of the thrill and shock of what is ungraspable. This applies to raptors, yes, but not only to raptors – I see other people's tastes and habits, now, through that lens of knowing and unknowing, my own self too. To look at nature is to look at ourselves as part of nature. Beholding that which we do not understand in the air may help us hold what is mysterious between us. Knowing has a purpose, in the pedagogy of this poem: not to conquer, but to witness.

I don't write as many letters as I used to, but I do write them occasionally. I even send some of them, but there are others I don't. Something happens for me when I address a letter to a 'you', even when I know nobody other than me will ever read what I've written. The address of 'you' draws feeling to the surface. Ideas find their locality, even in the one-sided conversation of an unsent letter.

Our written communications to each other – text messages, DMs, emails, postcards, voice notes, letters – remind us of how interpersonal we are. Relationships bring us to summits and valleys of love. Letters – perhaps especially in the first, never-to-be-sent drafts – contain much information. They speak back to their writer, asking to be heard.

Dear New Blood
Mark Turcotte

You don't need me, I know, here on this podium with
my poem. You hunched in the back of the room,
tilted in your lean reservation lean. You ho-hum your
gaze out the window toward some other sky.

Dear new blood, dear holy dear fully mixed up
mixed down mixed in and out blood, go ahead and
kick the shit, kiss the shit from my ears. I swear I
swear I'll listen. Stutter at stutter at me you uptown
weed you thorn you petal, aim my old flowered face
at the sky.

I know you don't need me, here on this podium with
my poem. You pressed flat to the wall, shoulders
cocked, loaded for *makwa*, for old growlers like me.
You yawn your glance out the window at the
tempting sky.

Wake me. Bang my dead drum drum, clang clang my
anvil my bell. Shout me hush me your song, your
shiny impossible, your long wounded song. Tell me
everything you know, you don't. Tell me, do you feel
conquered and occupied? Maybe I've forgotten. Sing
it plain, has America ever been America to you, let
you be you in your own sky?

Sing deep Chaco, deep Minneapolis, deep Standing Rock, deep Oakland and LA. Sing deep Red Cliff, sing Chicago, deep Acoma, deep Pine Ridge and Tahlequah. Sing and mourn. I think you, too, were born with broken heart. Rise. Smash your un-American throat against the edge of thereddening sky.

(*makwa*: Ojibwemowin for 'bear')

Mark Turcotte's 'Dear New Blood' takes the form of a letter addressed to an audience. It's an epistolary poem and the communication is filled with information, energy, assertion, history, ambition, survival, place and artistry. Did those to whom the letter was addressed ever read these words? I don't know. Could he have written this without the experience of the room and its sulky detractors? I don't think so. We affect each other in so many ways.

Who, or whose, is the 'New Blood' of the address and title? A specific audience, surely, but also a broader one. Mark Turcotte speaks directly, with a razor-sharp understanding that the resistance he experienced in the room was neither the only nor the deepest intuition of his listeners. He's 'on this podium with my poem' whereas his listeners – younger artists, I'm guessing – are 'hunched in the back of the room' looking 'out the window toward some other sky.' They are 'mixed up mixed down mixed in and out blood' and 'holy'. Though they gave every indication of wishing to not be in the room, the plain truth is that they are, nonetheless, there. They didn't leave. Could they have if they wished? Or is this a mandatory class? Sometimes I've chosen to occupy a room so that I can communicate my resistance. We are some subtle beings.

If – and it's a big if – the listeners, the 'New Blood' were in the room on the basis of their own free choice, then what we have is a clash of will: not the will of the listeners against the will of the poet; but the will of the listener to be there and not-there at the same time. Or maybe they don't wish to leave, but rather wish to be where the speaker is: 'on this podium with my poem.'

It can be hard to know what to do with desire. It compels us to go places that can be difficult to bear. The poet uses hunting language to describe his listeners: 'flat to the wall, shoulders cocked, loaded for *makwa*, for old growlers like me.' He understands he's the prey in the room hoping the hunters, hunched on their seats, will see game other than him. Desire, even complex desire, can provide a certain kind of comfort. This is understandable, but the probing nature of this epistolary poem asks its recipients to analyse their desire and examine if the comfort of resistance is serving them well.

Another person might have left this reading, saying disparaging things about resentful audiences. Predictable tropes about *the young* could have been projected, and what was not meant personally could have been taken personally. It's an easy trap to fall into. However, in the presence of a crowd whose ambition and ambivalence are present in equal measure, Mark Turcotte's response is one of generosity. This, then, is why the epistolary choice is so perfect for the poem: the form carries the message. 'Dear' he titles it, and addresses his listeners with kindness, understanding, clarity and focus. A letter speaks to its recipient directly, even naming them. Its work is in the receiving. 'Dear New Blood' is an appeal, a joining-together, through the medium of language. It asks for a response, like a communication to a friend. It is an act of solidarity and directs attention toward the true distress: the damaged ground.

What do they know about each other, this poet and the listeners? He seems older. And while he has more knowledge, he doesn't deliver it in the form of a lecture or reprimand: he makes a bridge of art, knowledge, shared pain and limitation. 'Tell me / everything you know, you don't.' We know things. We don't know things. We are. We aren't. The tumbling nature of the lines is an invitation to release. He invites the listeners to join their lament, their rage, their art, their creativity, their protest: 'Sing deep Chaco, deep Minneapolis, deep Standing Rock . . . Sing and mourn.'

'Dear New Blood' understands what thoughts might have gone through the minds of his audience, but also what emotions, and the language is chosen to echo and communicate on this level too. Lines such as 'go ahead and kick the shit, / kiss the shit from my ears' encapsulate and embrace ambivalence. The sound makes meaning too: from the explosion of the repeated 'k' to more repetition:

> Wake me. Bang my dead drum drum, clang clang my anvil my bell. Shout me hush me your song, your shiny impossible, your long, wounded song.

The knowledge that informs the syntax is evident: a feeling of being treated violently, of feeling worthless, of impending death and noise. Rather than attempt to defeat volume with more volume, a quieter tone is found: the desire for 'hush' in the midst of long trauma, the 'shiny impossible' hope for an adequate song. The acoustics of language form an emotionally intelligent onomatopoeia where the sound echoes the chaos experienced and the comfort desired.

It feels like Langston Hughes's famous poem 'Let America Be America Again' influences part of what's asked in 'Dear New Blood':

Tell me, do you feel conquered and occupied? Maybe I've forgotten. Sing it plain, has America ever been America to you, let you be you in your own sky?

Mark Turcotte is Turtle Mountain Anishinabe, and, writing about 'Dear New Blood', he recalls the power of poetry emerging from many young Native people. He describes how, in many of his readings, his younger listeners were 'bored but vibrating'. He recognises this himself, the mix of ambition and resistance: ambition in the arts, resistance to the America that has never let Indigenous people 'be you in your own sky'. Every stanza ends with this word 'sky' – that which surrounds, that which holds day, dawn, dusk, night, stars and clouds. That through which we discern horizon, and perhaps the direction of our prayer and yearning.

In the psychology of the poem, ambition and resistance are invited to a new sharpness: not to be directed against a visiting poet behind a podium, but honed for the purpose of making.

A friend told me that if he were a writer (he says he's not) he'd write a novel about a population of people who have no external catastrophe facing them.

What would happen in such a book? Would the characters, in the absence of outside suffering, create chaos among themselves? Are we capable of coping with relative ease?

My friend is neither an idealist nor a stranger to strain. In his idea, I hear curiosity about the philosophical, psychological and artistic question of whether we are able to actually be with each other, and the function of our relationship to pain.

The Uses of Sorrow

Mary Oliver

(In my sleep I dreamed this poem)

Someone I loved once gave me
a box full of darkness.

It took me years to understand
that this, too, was a gift.

Mary Oliver, who died in 2019 at the age of eighty-three, is one of the best-known poets in the United States. Many of her poems concern a relationship with the natural world: swans, geese, deer, lakes, trees, crickets and other insects. However, her interest in the natural world was not only in the seeming benevolence of it. She also portrayed the world as a place of morality, immorality and amorality, evidenced in her work exploring death, rage, predatory behaviour, illness, trauma, escape, religion and loneliness.

Mary Oliver spent forty years with her partner, Molly Malone Cook (1925–2005), and the 2006 collection *Thirst* in which 'The Uses of Sorrow' appears was dedicated to Cook's memory. This volume of her poetry – along with 'The Leaf and the Cloud' – is the one I know best. I've memorised some lines, been troubled by others, and navigated changes in my life with more. Ostensibly these couplets are about sorrow and its uses. It is a poem about time, too: 'It took me years to understand'. It is also about human connectedness and suffering, and what happens between people who love each other. However none of these are where I wish to begin – it's the strange epigraph-like statement that appears between the title and the twin couplets:

(In my sleep I dreamed this poem)

What is this? It's not a quote – no attribution is given. These seven words are contained within parenthesis; a word coming from Greek sources implying 'to put alongside/ beside'. Usually a bracketed remark adds something, although perhaps at an oblique angle, to the content of a sentence or paragraph. To bracket something can mean that the rest of the language *can* stand alone but is inadequate without what's communicated in the parentheses. Does Mary Oliver's inclusion constitute some critical distance that the speaker wishes us to maintain? Is it an instruction? Or a warning note that such insights come from a dreamplace where wisdom like this can be held without threat? Maybe it's a disclaimer, a note of self-consciousness to the suffering to say that any thought arrived from the unconscious world of sleep. The audacity of the title 'The Uses of Sorrow' requires some note of caution. The work is incomplete without these seven italicised words.

What of the body of the poem, and that 'box full of darkness'? Does this mean the darkness within which the world breathes? I suspect this box is a metaphor for some difficulty, given to her by someone she 'loved' – that past tense (not 'someone I love') allowing the blank space of the page to be filled with possibilities. What kind of gift did this turn out to be? And how many years did it take to realise 'that this, too, was a gift'?

For the last few minutes I have been chewing over the word 'once'. Is the 'once' lined to 'Someone I loved once'? Or is it that this person 'once gave me / a box full of darkness'? Of course the answer to this question is simple. Poetry. Yes. Both. And more. If the once is referring to a person – 'Someone I loved once' – then maybe that's the dream; perhaps in waking life this speaker never loved that someone.

It is too easy to speak easily of suffering. In bad literature, it's the crucible in which the character of a protagonist is refined. Mary Oliver suffered – that much is clear in her 2015 interview with Krista Tippett, one of the rare interviews the private poet gave. I've suffered. You as well. Millions upon millions – in fact, I should say *billions* – have suffered. I'm guessing few of us would *prescribe* it as a way to develop gratitude, or fortitude even though many of us would say that some of our suffering has led to deeper wisdom and understanding. Suffering is probably a fact of life, even though much hardship could be alleviated with some good leadership. Living and loving is difficult enough, without having to learn to live on the wrong side of policy, cruelty and neglect, but the eradication of such sufferings would not end pain. So, we must speak about suffering, but we must speak about it carefully. James Baldwin, in his essay 'Down at the Cross' reflects something similar: 'I do not mean to be sentimental about suffering . . . but people who cannot suffer can never grow up, can never discover who they are.' Perhaps his self-conscious 'I do not mean to be sentimental' functions in the same way that Mary Oliver's epigraph does.

In untrustworthy hands, the sentiments explored by 'The Uses of Sorrow' could justify the alienation and mistreatment of populations of people, so that *eventually* they too will discover the purpose of their suffering. This is abuse.

And yet, we live with complication – horror, even. How to live? With protest. With resistance. With art. With voting and working for change. With an inner life that does not give sanctuary to final hostility. I don't know how to write about suffering. I see the tensions inherent in this poem. And I see (though it's taken me years) as much bravery as risk in the composition of these lines.

When I meet people who think Mary Oliver's poetry is all *butterflies, bunnies, blah, blah, blah*, I wonder if they've read enough of her work. Not that anyone *should* like her poetry – anyone can like or dislike what they want, for whatever reason – but her knowledge of land, its animals and its fruit seems more about survival and subsistence than ease. However, I don't assume that this poem is a comment on factual details of Oliver's life, or personal philosophy. No matter what we know – or think we know – about her life, she may not be referring to circumstances of her own biography at all. In fact, the 'dream' could function as an instruction *against* reading these words as a comment about her own instinct, survival, or grief. In any case, we are all more than a balance sheet of achievements, pain, privileges and giftings. What else can be said? We are a strangeness to ourselves and each other. We must find ways to live alone and together, and the poem's title – 'The Uses of Sorrow' – styles itself as instruction rather than justification, explanation or confession. An instruction for what? For living: with the sorrows we have; the sorrows that last; the ones that ask (*demand!*) attention.

When I'm spiralling, or feeling derailed, I have a tendency to believe I can *think* my way out of whatever it is that's put me in a funk.

Usually, though, what actually helps is an interruption, a surprise, a moment of laughter, or an opportunity to help someone else. Forgetting about myself is a fine intervention. I'm glad for it, and try to arrange for it to happen – ridiculous as that seems – when I find myself falling into old patterns, yet again.

small talk or in my hand   galaxies

Benjamín Naka-Hasebe Kingsley

it looks like the thief rocketed
their whole self through
the bull's eye of my driver's side door
and you're not wrong to expect
the old joke about there being
nothing in my car worth the thieving
or maybe i've caught you eyerolling
please god not another
poem about windows but i cross my
fingers hope to die suck on diesel
and be hogtied i'll avoid simile
for the eye and soul and i'll be
careful as the fixer's hands
who came to pry waterlogged
lining from my inner door
her small boots crunching sun in the
glittered puddle of fractured glass
i think how i didn't think to sweep
but even so she is still kind i think
to get her a glass of tap water now
but then think of all the stairs
she says this big sol reminds her
of *cuba y tú* she asks but i don't
relish speaking spanish anymore
i tell her no i have always lived
here in miami i lie but offer my father
was a mason and bueno too at that
i've given her this one fractled truth as if
it could be understood not to mistake

my soft handshake for ignorance
of all the working classes but she
is not thinking of me only the door's
motor grinding she asks but what do i do
i hope she will ask
if maybe i am a mason myself but no
i say i am maybe a writer
me too she beams and offers a full palm
of what she'd vacuumed from the doorframe
shattered glass beads of blue refraction
wonder she says wonder at all they have
seen she insists ver toward the tiny eyelets
en mi mano galaxias she says and i wonder
how often i have mistaken myself
for the seer for the see-er
and others simply as the seen.

To give a poem two titles, such as Benjamín Naka-Hasebe Kingsley's 'small talk or in my hand⠀⠀galaxies' is to formally establish a poem of multiple meanings. The extra space between 'hand' and 'galaxies' invites even more speculation. Before I've read beyond the title, I am considering how 'small talk' could be a pathway to having space 'in my hand'. The scope expands from the immediate to the immense. No wonder there's a need for the visual breath before 'galaxies'.

A car has been burgled, 'the thief rocketed / their whole self through / the bull's eye of my driver's side door' (galaxies are explored by rockets, we are already seeing the links, even though he doesn't yet). But the speaker is less focused on his car and more interested in finding the right poetic techniques. He pre-empts an old joke 'about there being / nothing in my car worth the thieving' and wards off impatience from an intolerant reader who'd say 'please god not another / poem about windows'. This, then, is a poet whose car once had little value in it, but now has a broken window to boot. However, he's more worried about language, as he tries to communicate in a way that is neither predictable nor obvious. He's looking for a levity he can't place. Or perhaps he's hoping for validation: *am I writer? have I written the last best thing I'll write? can I even describe what's happening in front of me? Others can, I can't.* I wonder if this is someone who feels like he's not written in months.

Then along comes the fixer. The poet has been in his

head, but she is in her body, her whole self. It's her 'careful' hands we see first, and then 'her small boots crunching sun in the / glittered puddle of fractured glass'. He's wondering about getting her water, but fretting about the flights of stairs. She, however, is filled with easy conversation, making connections, drawing him out, talking about 'this big sol' and '*cuba*'. Her reply invites him out of himself, even though he's still in his head: 'i tell her no i have always lived / here in miami i lie but offer my father / was a mason and bueno too'. Not only is he anxious about finding the right language, he also doesn't want his 'soft handshake' to be mistaken 'for ignorance / of all the working classes'. She's content in her world, whereas he's trying to fit into his, unsure of his place. He's looking for poetic techniques, whereas she's finding them without looking for them.

I like both of them: I connect with his worry about writing well enough, as well as the perception of what a writer's life is like. I connect with her ease, her love of language, her recognition that trade and small talk are the stuff of wonder. Small talk – there it is. Often a derogatory term for insubstantive communication but she elevates it: 'she asks but what do i do' and even here, his self-consciousness re-emerges, his desire to be taken for 'a mason myself'. Somehow, he hears himself speaking the truth, revealing that he's a writer – the very thing he had been doubting. Her boots had crunched the sun in the glittered puddle, and now she 'beams' before seeing 'en mi mano galaxias'.

Is he attracted to her? Who wouldn't be? She's a light, a guide. She shows him what can be seen in work, in service, in trade, in language, in location, in query, in poetry, in exploring right where you are. He's divided in himself – 'i don't / relish speaking spanish anymore' – perhaps for good reason. She, whether she's divided or not, is present, and he experiences being seen by someone he'd not have expected to have felt seen by. What is so appealing about her is that she draws the self out in others, to be in her orbit is to shine with your own being.

She's shared language and curiosity and conversation and now she shares a handful of stars. He's caught in a funk of himself, and – it feels to me, but I'm probably projecting – he's trying to language his way out of a problem that language is causing. She's the defamiliarising surprise that awakens him. She combines 'small talk' and 'galaxies'. She's making art, and being made by it, possessed by it. And he, who had felt like poetry was far away from him, is also finding it right in front of him, like a muse.

It's easy to think this the beginning of a romantic sequence: either where they'd date, or one of them would want to. But the attraction is deeper than that. He's drawn into what draws her: the capacity to see, and in her gaze, his fractured broken self is not evidence of failure, but rather the possibility of how light can be refracted. There are verses throughout the ages addressed to a muse, someone who sparks the art in the poet. Distinct from that tradition, but nonetheless within it, not projecting otherworldliness onto the fixer, but seeing how she delights in the world, Benjamín Naka-Hasebe Kingsley's artistic problems are elevated into the stuff of proclamation by the end of 'small talk or in my hand   galaxies'.

If aliens were to land and demand that you encapsulate the human condition on a single page of writing (stay with me, I'm assuming these are aliens with literary curiosities), what would you say?

What local story would you use? What would you share that reveals the conflicted heart of humanity? What would you say about our planet, our past, and our relationship to resources? Do you have theories on humanity's capacity for – or resistance to – change? What mythologies would you use? What shape would you give your writing?

Species
Tishani Doshi

When it is time, we will herd into the bunker of the earth
to join the lost animals – pig-footed bandicoot, giant sea
snail, woolly mammoth. No sound of chainsaws, only
the soft swish swish of dead forests, pressing our heads
to the lake's floor, a blanket of leaves to make fossils
of our femurs and last suppers. In a million years
they will find and restore us to jungles of kapok.
Their children will rally to stare at ancestors.
Neanderthals in caves with paintings of the gnu
period. Papa *Homo erectus* forever squatting over
the thrill of fire. Their bastard offspring with prairie-size
mandibles, stuttering over the beginnings of speech. And finally,
us – diminutive species of *Homo*, not so wise, with our weak necks
and robo lovers, our cobalt-speckled lungs. Will it be for them
as it was for us, impossible to imagine oceans where there are now
mountains? Will they recognize their own story in the feather-tailed
dinosaur, stepping out of a wave of extinction to tread over blooms
of algae, never once thinking about asteroids or microbial stew?
If we could communicate, would we admit that intergalactic
colonization was never a sound plan? We should have learned
from the grass, humble in its abundance, offering food and shelter
wherever it spread. Instead, we stamped our feet like gods,
marveling at the life we made, imagining all of it to be ours.

Scattered throughout Tishani Doshi's urn-shaped 'Species' are references to time, space, change, and memory – all narrated in a voice that speaks of 'we' and 'they'. Where to begin? In time, of course, which is the first line: 'When it is time'.

When it is time for *what,* precisely? Human extinction seems to be the certitude in this shapely poem: it doesn't propose a possible 'if it comes to it' or 'it might be' – what it envisions is expected as an eventuality. Then 'we will herd into the bunker of the earth / to join the lost animals'. Even the verb 'herd' is telling. We will be like cattle, huddling together in meagre survival before inevitable extinction. But there's no promise here, just foretelling: 'When it is time'.

Doshi uses humour and hyperbole, centred form and fantastic language – 'pig-footed bandicoot, giant sea / snail, woolly mammoth' – alongside serious tones. 'Species' functions as a prediction and a warning, and nestled under its linguistic delights is the shock – or threat, or fact – of extinction. It is past time for paying attention, the speaker warns.

The sound of our machines will be silenced, and there will be no forests, just the 'soft swish swish' of dead ones; no water, just dry beds. And our futures will be found only in the fossils we form. The second sentence of this thirteen-sentence poem ends with 'last suppers', a reference to a meal marked in the Christian gospels which believers assert preceded a crucifixion and a resurrection. No resurrection here, just restoration in a science project in a million years, where we will be looked upon by the children of the future who will feel as distant from us as we feel from Neanderthals. Who are these people (if *people* is the right word) of the future? The perspective of these beings will see us 'with our weak necks / and robo lovers, our cobalt-speckled lungs' as early relations to – merely a 'bastard offspring' – those who discovered fire.

Once, awake in the middle of the night, I listened to a radio programme about science fiction. I don't know what the programme was called. But the presenter called attention to the fact that science fiction is often as much about the present as it is the future; that the fantastical projections of alien features – powers; weapons; pointy-eared, mind-reading laser-wielding extraterrestrials – are a distraction from what it is that such literature reveals about the present. This is the case in 'Species', whose very title is an examination of characteristic features of contemporary human behaviours: committed to the destruction of our planet and each other; pathologically immune to incontrovertible warning-signs; addicted to temporary pleasures at the expense of accountability; repeating patterns of the past that we already know brought doom. It isn't a pretty picture.

Speaking of picture, the shape of the poem asks for attention: the undulating line created down both the left and the right on the page suggests something. What is it? An aerial sketch of a spaceship? An urn for our ashes and imaginations? Some kind of misshapen egg-timer? Some vessel sufficient enough to save animals and nature and us? The lists of life in the poem includes not only the bandicoots, snails and mammoths but also forests, lakes, leaves, jungles, the gnu period, prairies, oceans, mountains, dino-saurs, blooms, algae and grass. I think of the Babylonian and Hebrew bible narratives of the Ark: a small preserving container, bearing the tasks of memory, lamentation or warning. The linguistic furniture of 'Species' may be deemed *apocalyptic*, but the theological training that I can't leave behind reminds me that a theology of apocalypse is – much like science fiction – less interested in foretelling the future than in revealing the present.

Some science fiction imagines exchanges between humans and aliens: whether hostilities, scientific discoveries, or deepening mutual understanding. However, 'Species' strips the question of such exchange back to a fundamental question: whether communication is possible:

If we could communicate, would we admit that intergalactic colonization was never a sound plan?

The second line stands alone. Suddenly fiction is absent, as is the future, and the present's relationship with colonial pasts is evoked. Can we communicate at all? What would it be like for a serious reckoning with the technologies – like empires – of the past? What would that look like? Listening, comprehending, and acting upon vital information, becoming the selves that our species needs us to be in order to survive.

The vital question emerges: even if we are interested in change, are we capable of it?

It is both a trope and a truth to state that the future is uncertain, but Tishani Doshi's lines 'When it is time' and 'we will' and 'no sound of' are unapologetically certain about some of the future. 'Species' depicts humanity as creatures who feel distant from even recently extinct realities, no less when we have been responsible for some of those extinctions. She sketches humanity's repeated tendencies to manifest attachments to escapism, destruction and nostalgia; a set of behaviours that elicits a damaged and damaging relationship with knowledge, self-preservation and conservation.

The site of education is not the *past*, but rhymes with it: 'We should have learned / from the grass'. What lessons would grass teach? Adapt; use available energy without destroying the source; provide nurture; share space with other growing breathing things; survive, even in harsh climates.

I worked as a school chaplain for a year. My boss told me my job consisted of helping young people to have positive experiences of sharing stories from their lives, as well as good interactions with each other, and that I should always welcome disagreement, especially about religion. Oh, she said, and learn everybody's name. Quickly. I don't care how you do it. Just do it.

Sometimes I think a poem is a difficult thing to write, but I've never worked harder in language – whether a soft response, or a careful question, or a word of affirmation or praise, or saying absolutely nothing – than in that job.

The Rungs

Benjamin Gucciardi

Only the person with the green dice should be talking,
I remind the boys, holding up the oversized foam cubes.

And the others should be? Listening, K. says,
and how should we listen? *Con el corazón*, M. replies,

thumping his chest with his closed fist.
That's right, I say, with the heart. Who wants to start?

The dice are passed around the circle
and the boys gloss over the check-in question.

When they reach B., who walked here, unaccompanied,
from Honduras three months ago, he holds them like boulders.

We straighten up when his lip begins to quiver.
It's not my place to tell you what he shared that day.

But I can tell you how M. put his hand on B.'s back
and said, *maje, desahógarte*,

which translates roughly to un-drown yourself,
though no English phrase so willingly accepts

that everyone has drowned, and that we can reverse that gasping,
expel the fluids from our lungs.

I sit quietly as the boys make, with their bodies, the rungs of a ladder,
and B. climbs up from the current, sits in the sun

for a few good minutes before he jumps back in.
The dice finish the round and we are well over time.

I resist the urge to speak about rafts, what it means to float.
Good, I tell them, let's go back to class.

After handshakes and side hugs, I'm left alone in the small room
with a box of unopened tissues, two starburst wrappers on the ground.

I've been in so many rooms where groupwork takes place; as a young person myself, or as a facilitator. Recognisable dynamics are present in most of these rooms: people sit in a circle; some want to be there, some don't; some are there because they have to be. There are always rules: 'Only the person with the green dice should be talking' the group leader says many times every week; and every group has a certain code, a shibboleth for belonging: 'how should we listen? *Con el corazón*'.

These rituals and practices are there to facilitate possibility. Many weeks feel like a slog – and I'm mostly thinking they'd feel like a slog to the young people who just want to get on with playing a game of football – but sometimes something happens, and the weeks of slog bear fruit. 'The Rungs' is such an experience where the groundwork routine supports the moment of possibility. Groupwork is the setting for this poem, and trust is the unfolding plot.

Benjamin Gucciardi founded an organisation – Soccer Without Borders – in 2006, and through it engages with newcomer youth in California. There's a small indication of the quality of his work – both as a poet and as a group leader – in the line:

The dice are passed around the circle
and the boys gloss over the check-in question.

I understand the mundanity of those check-in questions: things like 'If your mood today was a colour, what colour would it be?' or 'If you could describe your feelings today like weather, what's the weather like?' They're not awful, and maybe they serve a purpose, but I don't love them. Whatever the check-in question was on the day the events of 'The Rungs' occurred, the boys glossed over it, and what I notice is that the speaker of the poem doesn't labour the point, doesn't say *No, do what I say*. He's not incapable of repetition – those rituals of dice and reminders of speaking from the heart – but he is capable of letting the group go where it needs to go. He's guiding, not forcing.

What happens in a group is a result of what the people in the group choose to share, not necessarily the instructions of the leader. The leader can set up favourable conditions, but that doesn't guarantee anything. When B. speaks, the others listen. As readers, we are excluded – and rightly so – from the content of what was said; people's private stories are not for the purposes of art. 'The Rungs' is not an exploitation of someone's survival for entertainment or thrill, rather it is a praise poem, written from the point of view of an adult, about what a group of boys made happen in a room in between classes. Language is used to share and to shelter: M. responds to B. in Spanish. The speaker simply holds the open atmosphere of the room, establishes and maintains a culture of kindness, but mostly tries not to be in the way. He doesn't force the check-in questions, and he also holds back from pressing the metaphors: rafts, floating. What does he know about these things, which are realities, not metaphors, for the boys here? The room has become a place of temporary salve, and that's enough. 'Good, I tell them, let's go back to class' he says – like some retired God, watching creation make its own goodness happen.

To facilitate is to make something easy – *facilitate* comes from the French word *facile* meaning, among other things, ease. If a room of people need something facilitated it implies that there is support needed for the discussion of a complicated topic. Good facilitation often stands on a lot of advance work, building the possibility for a lasting process to unfold.

'I sit quietly as the boys make, with their bodies, the rungs of a ladder'. A ladder – from where, to where? Up from everything that threatens to drown you as you try to hold yourself together. 'The Rungs' speaks to the intelligence of body language: the corazón; that thump on the chest; the touch of hands on the green dice; the legs that walked – to the room, across borders – and the backs that straighten when someone's lips quiver. A hand placed on a back. Quietly there are many pairs of eyes too: people watching as someone holds a story in their body. B. 'sits in the sun // for a few good minutes'. What is this metaphor? The sun of being watched by the eyes of other boys who offer unconditional support. In this room rituals are acted out: 'handshakes and side hugs'; the sustaining process of bearing witness, in a classroom, green dice on the ground alongside a box of tissues and sweet wrappers.

The speaker doesn't use the metaphor of rafts – rightly so – but makes a point of telling us he doesn't use it. Why? Perhaps to let us know that he knows this laboured metaphor would fail, that a leadership role in a room doesn't translate into fluency about the circumstances of the participants' lives. What moves me most in the poem is the atmosphere of trust among the boys. They know each other, they can contain the frustration of being in a facilitated room, and can turn towards each other when it's needed. One of them knew that he could share, holding those dice 'like boulders' – weighty things that nobody should have to hold, heavy things that hopefully he can release, if only for a few minutes. The words love and trust do not occur anywhere in this short poem, but they're everywhere in it. The trust is shown between the boys as they turn up and put up with the process. Trust is seen in the sharing and listening. There's love in the touch of a hand on a friend's body, and the language by which they undrown each other: '*maje, desahógarte*'. Love is shown when the right person offers the right support. The work of facilitating a group like this is as difficult and as simple as it sounds, demanding consistency and humility, availability and observation.

And as the kids leave the room, with scraps on the floor, they trust it'll be there waiting for them when they return.

There are writers whose words set me alight. I find it hard to finish their books: part of me doesn't want the magic to end so I delay it; part of me is so captivated by their words that I can only get through a few pages at a time before needing to write.

What is this? Skill? Yes, presumably. It's something else too: some shared fire. I used to feel embarrassed when I felt this, like whatever I wrote could only ever be mimicry. Nowadays, I praise that flame.

The Boss of Me
Patricia Smith

In fifth grade I
was driven wild by you,
my teacher   Copper pixie
with light shining from beneath
it   Eyes giggling azure through
crinkled squint   I
let you rub my hair   I
let you probe the kinks   I
clutched you, buried my nose
in the sting starch of your white
blouses I asked you if you thought
I was smart did you know
how much I wanted to come
home with you to roll and cry on
what had to be a bone-colored
carpet I found out where
you lived I dressed in the morning
with you in mind I spelled huge
words for you I opened the dictionary
and started with A I wanted to
impress the want out of you
I didn't mind my skin because you
didn't mind my skin I opened big books
and read to you and watched TV news
and learned war and weather for you
I
needed you in me enough to take
home enough to make me stop rocking
my own bed at night enough

to ignore my daddy banging on the front door
and my mama not letting him in I
prayed first to God and then to you
first to God and then to you
then to you and next to God then
just to you
Mrs Carol
Baranowski do you even remember
the crack of surrender under your hand?
Do you remember my ankle socks
kissed with orange roses, socks turned perfectly
down and the click of the taps in my black
shiny shoes that were always pointed toward
you always walking your way always
dancing for a word from you? I looked
and looked for current that second
of flow between us but our oceans
were different   yours was wide and blue
and mine
was

Patricia Smith's 'The Boss of Me' is a praise song to Mrs Carol Baranowski, a teacher who was a fixation – a term sometimes associated negatively, but here it's something like salvation – for a pupil. Mrs Carol Baronowski's hair ('Copper pixie'), eyes ('azure') and clothing ('the sting starch of your white / blouses') are all tangible and adored. Her home had been imagined and then 'I found out where / you lived'. The title – 'The Boss of Me' – evokes a speaker who has found someone worthy of her love and submission. Could the teacher have borne such love had it ever been expressed? Could the child have borne the communication, or rejection, of such love? We are so filled with hunger.

This teacher is better than God:

I
prayed first to God and then to you
first to God and then to you
then to you and next to God then
just to you

Why? Because she was there, responding, educating, inspiring, correcting. She was touchable and touching, even past boundaries: 'I / let you rub my hair   I / let you probe the kinks   I / clutched you, buried my nose / in [you]'.

Worship is etymologically linked to worth and this woman with '[e]yes giggling azure through / crinkled squint' was worthy of love. To love her was to be loved back into being. The single word 'I' occurs seventeen times, five times at a line's end, and once as the single word on a line of its own. The attention given to the teacher allowed the student – a child who knew 'my daddy banging on the front door / and my mama not letting him in' – to flourish. The educator was good enough to be the focus of a pupil's love, but paradoxically, the love was not just for the teacher, rather it was a nascent love of the student for their own life. 'I asked you if you thought / I was smart'. Patricia Smith – she speaks warmly of how autobiographical this poem is – knew she was intelligent but needed to hear it from someone else who also saw it. Under such a gaze, she expanded:

> I spelled huge
> words for you I opened the dictionary
> and started with *A*
>
> . . .
>
> I opened big books
> and read to you and watched TV news
> and learned war and weather for you

She experienced something of citizenship: in her own life, her classroom, her mind and creativity.

I was lucky to have such adults in my life. Ruth Maybury and I shared a birthday, and when I wrote letters to her, she replied. Ray Murphy – I thought he was so old, but he was only twenty-five – taught me the guitar. Aldo Magliocco was a Belfast man with an Italian name whose ease and kindness was a balm in complicated years. When I heard he died, only in his early fifties, I walked miles in Manhattan with rain diluting my tears. As an eleven-year-old I noticed, and copied, the handwriting of Colin Green. Decades later, far away from Ireland, I was in a meeting and someone said 'My name is Colin Green' and I instantly knew why I'd not been able to take my eyes off him. We reconnected and are still in touch. No parent is enough, and love comes from many sources. It needs to.

'I didn't mind my skin because you / didn't mind my skin'. Alongside Patricia Smith's childhood devotion to her teacher is the recognition of their dissimilarity. The 'white / blouses' and 'what had to be a bone-colored / carpet' locate the distinctions in objects. Between a white teacher and her Black student from the west side of Chicago there are racial, cultural and historical differences. Perhaps this also goes some way to explain the conclusion, if it can be called that: 'yours was wide and blue / and mine / was'. The abrupt ending leaves the reader in the unbridged gap of what is not narrated, what was not said, the message that does not know if it ever reached its addressee.

I interviewed Patricia Smith at the Geraldine R. Dodge Poetry Festival a few years ago. She spoke of how she'd never been able to trace her beloved teacher, so the poem acts as a voice of praise to all teachers deserving of such adulation. Mrs Baranowski saw in the young student what her family didn't see, and urged the poetry out of her, allowing her to locate herself in the here-and-now, even though the here-and-now was a place that evoked fantasies of escape in the child. Writing was her way to engage safely with a world she couldn't leave. And when she did finally leave, she brought writing with her, having honed it by responding to her teacher's repeated – and sometimes illogical – questions: *What sound does that colour make? How does that colour taste? If that home had a voice, what would it sound like?* It was by such close attention that writing sharpened.

Studying phenomenology a few years ago, I was relieved to read philosophers who assert that nobody knows what 'being' is. According to some, you need to stand apart from an experience to describe it objectively, and we are not capable of standing outside existence in order to explore what existence means. All of this is to consider the sense of self that arose in Patricia Smith: what caused it? Why that teacher, at that time? Could she have heard herself by any other means? I don't know the answer to these questions, and it's impossible to step outside of what happened to imagine if it could have happened in another way. What this leaves us with, then, is a song of praise for the salvation that did break in, not through divine intervention, but through someone who made her want to be herself. All stand. All praise Mrs Carol Baranowski.

In the realm of human interaction, the word 'resentment' has a bad reputation. And yet its etymology reveals riches: re-sentiment, to feel again. Feelings are powerful, sometimes overwhelming. Feelings fuel action and beliefs and the capacity to achieve insurmountable goals. Some of those goals are good. Sometimes abhorrent feelings give us agency and enterprise – whether for creative or destructive purposes. To resent, then, may be necessary: a stark reminder of what feelings can do if they are not examined for all their power and potential.

[*Non omnis moriar*]
Zuzanna Ginczanka

> Non omnis moriar multaque pars mei
> vitabit Libitinam
>
> Horace, Ode 3, 30

Non omnis moriar – my magnificent estate,
tablecloth meadows, steadfast fortress shelves,
my precious comforters and billowing sheets,
my dresses, my colorful dresses will survive.
I leave no heirs, so may your hand dig out
my Jewish things, Chominowa of Lvov, mother
of a Volksdeutscher, snitch's wife, swift snout.
May they serve you and yours, not any others.
My dears, this is no lute nor empty name,
I remember you, as you remembered me,
particularly when the Schupo came,
and carefully reminded them of me.
May my friends gather, sit and raise their glasses,
drink to my funeral and to their own rich gain –
carpets and tapestries, china, fine brasses –
drink throughout the night, and come the dawn
begin their mad hunt – under sofas and rugs,
in quilts and mattresses – for gems and gold.
O how the work will burn in their hands: plugs
of tangled horsehair and soft tufts of wool,
storms of burst pillows, clouds of goose down
will stick to their arms and turn them into wings;

my blood will seal the fresh feathers with oakum,
transforming birds of prey into sudden angels.

Translation by Alissa Valles

The poet Zuzanna Ginczanka was murdered by the Gestapo in her twenties. The exact date of her death is not known: sometime around the end of 1944 or the start of 1945. This untitled poem – her last – is one of her best known. In its powerful lines, we encounter a writer who animates contemporary occurrences with references from antiquity, here using a quote from the Roman lyric poet Horace to speak about poetry that survives death.

'Non omnis moriar multaque pars mei vitabit Libitinam' translates as 'not all that I am will perish, some of me will escape Libitna [the ancient Greek deity for burials, funerals and corpses]'. The original context for this line is Horace, surveying his *Odes* (this line comes from the third such volume) and reckoning that even after his death, his work will survive. It demonstrates his somewhat pompous sense of self-importance. Sometimes, in the face of such presumption, I'm annoyed that the ancient poets are correct, because here I am, thousands of years later, reading the guy who imagined his poems would survive him. But it's a temporary annoyance: first because Horace (and the others) wrote brilliantly, and second because the desire for legacy is such a widespread concern. It gives comfort to many to hope that a reputation, or children, or work, or kindness will – in little or large ways – bear witness to them after their death.

This, then, is what Zuzanna Ginczanka turned to on the descent to her murder by the Gestapo in Kraków. Already recognised as an important poet, her work contained fire and flight, tenderness and scalpel, rage and wonder. She spoke Russian and Polish, but chose to write in Polish and is renowned in her home country. Her work is alive with attention; in it we see whales, eagles, floods, and blood-stained fur; virginity, language, shock, and sensuality. Reading her poems, I experience many things: rage, amazement, admiration. I see how art coursed through her, and how her words attest to her interests, artistic dexterity, and determination to succeed.

All of this, then, concealed like a sharp blade in this untitled work. She faces death, and what will survive?

> my magnificent estate,
> tablecloth meadows, steadfast fortress shelves,
> my precious comforters and billowing sheets,
> my dresses, my colorful dresses will survive.

Zuzanna Ginczanka did not survive – she was only twenty-six when she was executed, either by a firing squad or a single shooter. She knew that her enemies would eventually die too, their snitching would not ensure survival.

What does she do in the dreadful and tortuous approach to this death? She writes. She tells the truth: what will remain are some of her things, but she will leave language behind that will continue to detail events as they occurred. Ginczanka had been arrested as a result of betrayal: she recalls in the poem how Chominowa gave up her hiding place. She did at first manage to escape. This was 1942, and while accounts of how she managed it are varied, she survived pursuit and persecution for another few years, until a subsequent capture that led to her execution.

I leave no heirs, so may your hand dig out
my Jewish things, Chominowa of Lvov, mother
of a Volksdeutscher, snitch's wife, swift snout.

In the face of her impending death, Ginczanka declares
herself and her possessions by their identity that was so
abhorred by those who hated Jews. She leaves a speech act
for the future: naming the woman who had given her up
those years before, a woman from Lvov, a mother, a wife,
together with her family. What is this? An act of revenge? If
so, it's a timeless one. Alissa Valles – the translator – includes
and comments on this poem in the introduction to her recent
NYRB translation of Ginczanka's work into English,
describing '[*Non omnis moriar*]' as being 'hurled across
time, both a testament and a curse.' Naming the family of
Chominowa, a husband, a wife, a son – 'a Volksdeutscher'
– the satire of the lyric demonstrates enduring energies: the
demand for accountability, for truth to be known, for some
kind of justice to be recognisable, even in a future the poet
is about to be obliterated from.

'My dears', she addresses her denunciators, before imag-
ining a scene where they can 'drink to my funeral and to
their own rich gain', surrounded by finery, yet still dissatis-
fied. Antisemitic caricatures of wealth had been heaped
upon European Jews as a justification for the murderous
greed of those who exterminated them. In her final work,
Ginczanka portrays the malcontentment of her condemners:
their lusts unabated, consumed, still, in a 'mad hunt'. She
whose people had been accused of greed now shows the
economy from which such false accusations arose: the
'horsehair' and 'tufts of wool' and 'burst pillows' and 'goose

down' stolen by her condemners in an attempt to transform themselves from 'birds of prey into sudden angels'.

Why angels? What kind of sentiment is this? Is she giving the accusers what they say they want, the appearance of innocence – surely nothing is as pure as an angel? Ginczanka portrays the hollowness of her haters' desire, depicting them as birds of prey who wish to cover their predatory nature, pasting their plumage with inept disguises, covered in the blood of someone they have damned. The scene is violent, macabre, over the top, the stuff of exaggeration and hyperbole. Yet this is no hyperbole; reality is worse. A young person is about to be murdered and she knows it. Those who conspired in justifying her extermination – and that of millions of others – did so for purposes of hatred, material gain, scapegoating and the ridiculous affectation of purity.

'I remember you' the poet writes from the grave, in twenty-four lines whose strength demonstrates the dexterity of her skill. Deservedly shaming as it is for colluders to be named, Zuzanna Ginczanka's name remains more memorable, for her witnessing, capacity and craft. This poem is a denunciation of all who colluded in the persecution and murder of her fellow Jews, and is also a renunciation of meekness. In this fighting till the end, and even further, in this publication even after perishing, part of her has escaped Libitna.

I didn't love my childhood years. One of the legacies of that time in my life is how quickly I still assume that everything is my fault. To have been told you're the problem means that believing you're the problem is a known place. I wish this were not the case. I know I am far from alone in this.

What helps? Many things: friends, humour, learning, support. What also helps? The daring act of making: a poem, a change, a surprising sound of new language where old language fails. Discovering a poem.

How the Dung Beetle Finds Its Way Home
Eugenia Leigh

The Milky Way's glinting ribbon helps the dung beetle
roll his good ball of shit back to the ones he loves.
But blind him to the sky with as little as a hat,
and he will swerve like a drunk who, if he makes it home alive,

might find the family, soured with waiting,
gone. Drawers cleared, beds cold, even the watercolor ark
of giraffes and raptors pulled from the face of the fridge.
See? I want to tell my missing father, it's a metaphor so simple

it's almost not worth writing down: even beetles need the stars
to nudge them back to where they need to be
when they need to be there – toward their little ones'
gummy grins ever pardoning the grisliest parent.

I am thirty-four with a son the day my mother tells me
she enrolled in a four-day seminar about how to be a good mom.
A little late, I know.
Once, in a rage, I left my husband and our sleeping child.

Where did you go, friends ask when I tell the story.
I wish I'd had a grander plan. I wish I'd stood on the roof
of our building and, empowered by that single Brooklyn star,
I'd ripped up the book of my parents' sins.

Or I wish I could tell someone the truth: that I fear
I am the kind of woman who could leave the one good family
God had the gall to give her. Really,
I sat on the stairwell leading up to the roof and wept

until a large bug threatened my life, at which point I recalled
the dung beetles, stopped blaming my parents, and –
thanking the metaphorical stars – I rolled up my pile of shit
and trudged back home.

As a result of Eugenia Leigh's 'How the Dung Beetle Finds Its Way Home' I've spent more time learning about shit-rolling insects than I ever thought I would. I'm glad though: the presence of this small being – and its relationship with the Milky Way – deepens the poem, and the poem deepens my life.

A dung beetle does what may be expected from an insect of that name: it spends time around excrement. Some, known as *rollers*, roll dung into round balls; others burrow the dung in tunnels – they're known as *tunnellers* – and others dwell in the dung; they're known, unsurprisingly, as *dwellers*. Some dung beetles are able to plot pathways home using the Milky Way. They're not known as *milkywayers* yet, as far as I know.

Leigh is self-conscious about the poem's use of metaphor:

> it's a metaphor so simple
>
> it's almost not worth writing down: even beetles need the stars
> to nudge them back to where they need to be
> when they need to be there . . .

Metaphor arises again at the conclusion: 'thanking the metaphorical stars – I rolled up my pile of shit / and trudged back home.' Why this metaphor, and why the attention to the device? Jacques Lacan, the French psychoanalyst, said that metaphor defies what language veils. In that analysis, the metaphor of the very stars in the sky being that which guides a parent insect home 'toward their little ones' / gummy grins ever pardoning the grisliest parent' addresses what is difficult to say: she knew abandonment, and her own forgiving grin wasn't enough to entice one parent home or the other towards health. Across her work, Leigh details parts of her mother's abusive behaviour, and explores how this contributed to her own adult experiences of post-traumatic stress. She lives with bipolar disorder – in fact, her collection is titled *Bianca*, the name her family called her when she was in a swing of mania. The humour, the delight, the natural wonder of the beetle who can navigate its way home is the plain telling of a truth addressed to her own parents: don't treat your children like shit; if even a beetle can provide for its family, so can you.

The speaker has found herself having left – very tempo-rarily – her home: 'Once, in a rage, I left my husband and our sleeping child.' History repeats itself. This is a good home, one that's worth returning to. Her fear is that she could be 'the kind of woman who could leave the one good family . . .' Leigh does not wish to flee her family, rather she's worried herself into imagining they'd want to be free of her, or better off without her. To be deceived by your own thinking is part of the legacy of pain. In the acknowledgements Eugenia talks of what it's like 'to hate your own brain'. She is seeking a pathway back: downstairs to her loving family, but also back to thinking that serves, rather than under-mines, her. She'd 'sat on the stairwell leading up to the roof and wept'. She was seeking a vehicle – a metaphor – to help her hold herself together, to return to the gift of a safe home, and bear with the complication of living with her own shit. The beetle provided this.

I love the insight into the speaker's relationship with her friends: '*Where did you go*, friends ask when I tell the story.' This is a life of someone who has a good husband, a son, friends, and also the capacity to speak aloud what might feel like a source of secrecy, shame and blame: *I parented in a way I didn't think I would*. I'm moved by the storytelling and the friendships, the exchanges of humour and confession that underpin the health of the poem and the poet's constellation of community.

'Good' is repeated three times: 'good ball of shit'; 'I am thirty-four with a son the day my mother tells me / she enrolled in a four-day seminar about how to be a good mom' and the 'one good family / God had the gall to give her'. That her own mother had not been a good one is evident, even from the mother's words: '*A little late, I know.*' Now, in a good family, the poet is facing the truth that goodness can be hard to bear when you've spent years feeling far away from it. To arrive at that which you've desired. To learn how to hold the thing you've always said you wanted. My god, it's hard. So many of us have done this: repeating old patterns of survival in the places where flourishing finally occurs.

The poem resolves, like some poems do. The poet finds it within her to return to the goodness that was so hard to bear, knowing that living with self may be the most difficult relationship. The long-ago invades today. The old haunts the new. The lies we believe even though we know they're lies. The weight of shame, and its awful rhyming partner, blame. She knows this rut, and that it leads nowhere, but she also needs the support of language, art, and visual metaphor to find her way out. In Leigh's hands, the turning volta isn't merely a poetic device, it's a social intelligence to be employed in the right circumstances.

The speaker didn't climb to the roof to stare at the stars and remember their navigational system. Instead, she was visited – 'a large bug threatened my life' – and she remembered the dung beetle, the Milky Way, and found the wherewithal to plot her own: the home she shares with people she loves, the stories she's able to tell to friends, the questions they'll ask, the capacity she's clearly built to thrive, the love she bears and brings, the way the new can feel impossible to carry, especially when the new feels good.

Communication, I learnt during group-work courses, is when a message is understood with its original intent.

That's a complicated thing to achieve: intentions are sometimes best left unvoiced; my intentions can been pretty limited, and in need of serious change.

On My Return from a Business Trip

John Lee Clark

Let go of my arm. I will not wait
until I'm the last person on the plane.
Go away. I never asked for assistance.
What? I don't want that wheelchair.
I'm fine. Let me walk.
Let me feel the spring
of my fiberglass cane off the walls.
What? I don't want the elevator.
Leave me alone. I don't know what color
my bag is and I don't care.
No, it won't take forever.
Go away. I'm fine kneeling here.
No. No. Yes. See?
I told you it wouldn't take forever.
Now will you please go away?
What? I'm just waiting, like you.
Let me feel the air get sucked away
just before the shuttle pushes it back.
No need, no need. I can step off
by myself. Let me go. Let me go home.
Go away. Let me walk
with my bag rolling behind me in the sun.
Let me veer off here
onto the grass. No, I'm not lost.
Go away so I can find out
whether it's indeed spring.

In John Lee Clark's 'On My Return from a Business Trip' we hear one half of a conversation. In sentences as clear as 'Go away', 'I'm fine', 'No', 'Leave me alone' and 'See?' details emerge of a single incident in which the speaker disembarks a plane, gathers luggage and makes their way home. A single incident? It's narrated as such, but the tone of the language implies that this happens often. A DeafBlind poet and essayist, John Lee Clark is also an advocate for the Protactile movement: a language among DeafBlind people, but also a philosophy that asserts independence and autonomy.

The title – 'On My Return from a Business Trip' – instructs the reader about the set-up. Someone has been on a work trip. He is clear, in communication and movement. He knows what he's doing, where he's going, and how to make his way. He understands – all too well – how assumptions will be made. This speaker is used to his arm being taken against his will: 'I never asked for assistance'. A wheelchair is offered, even though none is required. And his competence is questioned, even though it's clear he's making his way with a walking device just perfectly: 'Let me feel the spring / of my fiberglass cane off the walls.' He doesn't wish to take the elevator, taking instead (we presume) the stairs, and this prompts more offers of assistance, bringing the second 'What?' of the poem. Waiting for a checked bag to come out on the carousel, someone seems to have asked what colour it will be. 'I don't know what color / my bag is and I don't care . . . I'm fine kneeling here.' Then, with irony, 'See? / I told you it wouldn't take forever.'

There's nothing helpless about the speaker. It's clear that if he wanted help, he'd ask for it. 'I never asked for assistance.' And it is his assertions of independence that are deemed unbelievable. He's travelling for work, boarding planes, leaving them, taking stairs or escalators, waiting for and recognising his bags, taking buses, walking, pulling a suitcase behind him. What's being revealed is not that he's hostile to help; it's just that he doesn't need it. What is also revealed is the presumptive undercurrent of offers of help: I know enough about this person's dependence and ability to assume my offers are necessary, even against all evidence to the contrary.

I am not DeafBlind. I have not lived a life in which assumptions are made about my ability every time I go out. As I read 'On My Return from a Business Trip' I internalise its message. It's not *never offer any help to anyone*; rather, it's about remembering the necessity to ask myself a series of questions when I am seized by the impulse to offer: is the person asking for help? Am I assuming they need help based on my projections of need onto them? Is my help a denial of their autonomy?

The other day I was thinking about this poem as I took a train. Going up the stairs from the subway, someone seemed to be struggling. I wondered what I should do, if my assistance would be helpful, or simply a demonstration of my presumption that this person's presence in the world was an occasion for my interruption. I asked myself some questions. What else would my offer to help communicate? What if they really needed help? What if I were the one who needed to ask myself questions about my help? I was glad for the presence of the poem as I climbed the stairs. It isn't a new thought for me – that offers of help aren't always helpful – but it's an important reminder.

I see the three-times repeated 'What?' as a demonstration of how help can sometimes come in a language that is both unnecessary but also incomprehensible. Three times the word 'you' is repeated too:

> I told you it wouldn't take forever.
> Now will you please go away?
> What? I'm just waiting, like you.

Three lines held together by repetition of address. Repetition, too, of a message: *believe me* when I tell you I know what I'm doing and that your attention to me is not as supportive as you wish it to be.

'On My Return from a Business Trip' is included in a volume titled *How to Communicate* – a collection whose authoritative title demonstrates clarity and a specific role: instructor, not ignorant; able, not unable; independent, not reliant. Communication is two-way, we often hear in HR training at work, or messages about dialogue or politics or difference. Here, I am reminded of the necessity of accepting the communication that's coming my way, especially in the face of loud assumptions of mine that may belittle, no matter what my intentions. The tone in the poem is one of pushback, of *help yourself, not me*. A poem that states how offers of help are unhelpful is, ironically, one that helps: only the speaker isn't the recipient of such help, he's the donor. There is a message, an education, a simple lesson here: if I'm not asking for help, it means I don't need it.

This is a poem expressing the desire of one person, speaking for himself. While others may state their wishes differently, I am struck by the statement's power of voice and intention. When I read this poem, I think of how I hate it when assumptions are made about me, and yet, how fixed I can be on what I think a solution may be when I'm the one offering help. 'No need, no need,' I repeat to myself. 'Go away so I can find out' echoes, too: find out what? John Lee Clark wishes to find out simply if 'it's indeed spring.' A specific, tangible desire, but I also love the time-orientation of this final line's seasonal reference: it's about a man wanting to have his own time to himself, to approach things in his own way, and also to measure the reality of whether change has actually occurred.

How do we write about all that war takes? In many ways. Some people write elegies. Some write of rage. Some write fantasies about how things could have been. Others dig up ghosts whose wisdom is sore missed. There isn't a single way. Rather, every way can be a reminder of the difficult path out of war, and towards that ever-demanding hope: peace in a place that's become accustomed to the opposite.

Ibrahim Abu Lughod and Brother in Yaffa
Mosab Abu Toha

The two walk toward the beach,
barefoot.

With his soft
index finger,
Ibrahim starts to draw
a map
of what
used to be
their home.

'No, Ibrahim, the kitchen
is a little farther to the north.
Oh, don't step over there,
Dad was sleeping there on the couch.'

Tourist kids run by,
flying kites.
The waves hit
the beach,
shaded with cloud cover.

The mosque on the hilltop
calls for
prayer.

Ibrahim and his brother
still argue about where their kitchen was.
They both sit on the sand. Ibrahim
takes out a lighter, wishes he could make tea in their kitchen
for everyone on the beach.
Ibrahim looks upward to what used to be their kitchen window.
The mint no longer grows.

'The two walk toward the beach,' Mosab Abu Toha begins. From the title, we already know the names and location of the two characters: 'Ibrahim Abu Lughod and Brother in Jaffa'. Why are they walking *toward* the beach? A demonstration of ease, perhaps; a shared amble. Where are they walking from? The more I think about it, the more I think *memory* might be an answer.

The tone of these musical lines is easy: the brothers are barefoot, one draws on the sand with a 'soft / index finger', another urges the other not to wake their sleeping father, laid out on the couch of a house no longer there. The soundtrack is pleasant too: the chatter of kids and tourists, the rhythm of waves. Even the light is gentle – 'shaded with cloud cover'. This builds an appealing affect: the reader is invited into a place of memory, where brothers seek to recreate their home. For what? There may be many answers, but one of them is clear: 'tea in their kitchen / for everyone on the beach.'

Ibrahim Abu Lughod, the only named brother in the poem, was born in 1929 in Yaffa, in what was then British Mandate Palestine. He fled in 1948 as the state of Israel was being established, going initially to Beirut before settling in the US. He dedicated his life to cultural and democratic causes for Palestinian statehood and is credited with having significantly influenced US political and popular understanding of Middle Eastern affairs. Many years after his departure, he returned to his homeland – with an American passport – and after he died in 2001 he eventually did return to Yaffa: he's buried there. The ghosts of the brothers speak to each other about a home they still miss, even in death. Mosab Abu Toha's book *Things You May Find Hidden in My Ear: Poems from Gaza* was released in 2022, the year he turned thirty. He's the founder of the Edward Said Library in Gaza; Said being a close collaborator with Abu Lughod: the poem's source and setting is a meeting place of Palestinian authors. As I see Ibrahim Abu Lughod and his brother on the beach in Abu Toha's elegiac hymn, it's clear that a house is not the only presence being called back from the past: the statesman is also summoned as a figure of memory, hospitality, clarity and justice.

A dream, then? Are dreams naïve? I always baulk at the idea that *naïve* is an insult: the word comes from the Latin *nativus*, meaning original, natural, native, also related to *nātus*, implying born, begotten, birthed. Wasn't every thriving thing small once? Every idea, every possibility of safety? I write this in early 2024, as the death toll in Gaza – since the war in response to Hamas' murder of 1,200 Jews and kidnap of hundreds more – has topped 30,000. This is a nightmare, which is another kind of dream. How does anyone write poetry during a time of war? Will it be accused of being misleading, capitulating, pandering? In the choice between hell and whatever the imaginative possibility a dream of restoration and hospitality might offer, I'll turn my attention to what is being born. Slaughter's plot is predictable; birth's possibilities are latent.

For a while I thought the distant sound of the mosque in the poem was background noise, pleasant but unattended to. Now, though, I read the entire poem as a speech act of prayer, a demonstration of faithfulness and remembrance, obeisance paid to the sacred ground where absence is met with hospitable devotion. While the postures of prayer are not described, the body is: feet 'walk' and are 'barefoot' and that 'soft / index finger' draws in the sand; children run, brothers sit, one uses his hands to take out a lighter, and then 'looks upward'. The body in motion is alive, free. I think of the 'kite', the 'home', the 'mosque' and the 'couch' as objects placed throughout the six rooms of this poem: images of levity, welcome, devotion and rest. Objects, too, of culture, ease and ownership: safe citizenship rests in tangibility.

Gentle as the exchange is, control and consideration are uppermost in this exchange between two brothers who can talk and argue easily: 'don't step over there' is an imperative of love, not threat. Their father's resting space asks for courtesy not clamour.

Time is marked deliberately and powerfully by the use of tenses, a word that refers to past or present or future (among others) but also a term that speaks of tension: things stretched. We feel the tension between what was, what is not, what's hoped for, what's possible or not possible via the seemingly simple conjugations of time in the phrases 'the kitchen / is', 'where their kitchen was' and 'what used to be their kitchen window'.

Back, then, to the kitchen. The grief of the final line – 'The mint no longer grows' – is in contrast to the desire to 'make tea in their kitchen / for everyone on the beach.' For the tourist kids? Yes. But for others too: the living and the dead. The lighter's aim is to kindle a kettle, a kettle in *'their* kitchen' (emphasis mine). 'Ibrahim Abu Lughod and Brother in Jaffa' dreams that hospitality can coexist alongside restoration: of a house, of a family who never had to flee, of safety enough to walk to the beach. Earlier, we heard the brother assert:

> No, Ibrahim, the kitchen
> is a little farther to the north

Note the timestamp: *is*, not *was*. The past is still alive, and in the demands of the present, the desire is for a place for taking tea together, a place of belonging with belongings, where home and movement are not just the stuff of dreams. Is this a poem of ghosts on a beach reminiscing about the irrecoverable past? Or the dream of a place – by water – where hospitality and justice can be imaginable? I read it as the latter, because the nightmare is so much worse, and there are already too many elegies to be written.

On a work team in my late teens, everyone talked about our team's *disunity*. It was such an accepted description of our group that it went unquestioned, and much was explained by referring to our dysfunctional dynamic.

In time, someone new joined our group, and was quickly – off-stage – informed about our team's problem. The next time we had a meeting, someone spoke of our fractured group, and the new member said 'I think that's bullshit.'

Something broke; something was made; something new. I learnt a lot about what free language can do.

Waiting for the Barbarians
C.P. Cavafy

— Why are we waiting in the agora?

　　　　Because the barbarians arrive today.

— Why is there such uncertainty in the Senate?
　Why do the Senators sit there and not legislate?

　　　　Because the barbarians arrive today.
　　　　What laws can our Senators enact now?
　　　　The barbarians will legislate when they arrive.

— Why has our emperor awoken so early
　and seated himself before the city's main gate,
　on his throne, solemn, wearing his crown?

　　　　Because the barbarians arrive today
　　　　and the emperor wants us to greet
　　　　their leader. As is the custom, he will
　　　　present him with a parchment.
　　　　Many titles and names are written on it.

— Why have our two consuls and the praetors chosen
　today to don their red, embroidered togas?
　Why are they wearing bracelets adorned with amethyst
　and rings with shiny, glistening emeralds?
　Why do they carry expensive walking sticks
　gilded and inlaid with silver?

Because the barbarians arrive today,
and such things impress barbarians.

— And why have our outspoken orators not come as always
to spout their words, to have their say?

Because the barbarians arrive today
and eloquence and speeches bore them.

— Where has this anxiousness and confusion come from
all of a sudden? Look at the haunted faces.
Why are the streets and squares emptying so rapidly
and everyone returning to their homes so worried?

Because night fell and the barbarians never arrived.
Some men travelled to the border region,
and reported that the barbarians no longer exist.

————

Now what will we do without the barbarians?
They were a sort of solution for us.

Translation by Evan Jones

C. P. Cavafy's parable-like poem, translated from Greek to English by Evan Jones, is set in an undefined location, and poses strategic questions about leadership, fear, manipulation, inaction and democracy. Born in what was then Ottoman Egypt in 1863, Cavafy wrote 'Waiting for the Barbarians' in 1898. He published little in his lifetime, mostly in pamphlets distributed to acquaintances and contacts, but this particular work – one of his best known – was circulated in the early 1900s.

The poem is structured as a series of questions and answers: an observer poses questions and is answered by a knowledgeable interlocutor. In the original Greek poem, the questions were composed in fifteen-syllable sentences with the responses coming mostly in lines of twelve or thirteen syllables. In the voices of these two characters, then, a civic scene unfolds: a crowd is gathered in the agora – a place for assembly. This crowd's emperor is 'seated . . . before the city's main gate, / on his throne, solemn, wearing his crown' and before this bejeweled emperor, a city has come to an anxious quiet as theatre threatens to unfold. It isn't only the emperor who is outfitted finely: the consuls and praetors (officers), too, wear 'red, embroidered togas' and 'bracelets adorned with amethyst / and rings with shiny, glistening emeralds'. While the story is that everyone is 'waiting for the barbarians' it is equally true that the people (who wear 'haunted faces') are assembled to observe

Leadership in Costume. Seeing the scene, many questions suggest themselves: what's the play? Who is writing the script? Who is directing it? What's being achieved through this spectacle? What else is happening behind the scenes? Who is benefitting from this performance?

Notably the orators – described as 'outspoken', people who 'spout their words, to have their say'– are absent. Who has named them thus? And why are they not there, as they 'always' are? Are they imprisoned, or otherwise silenced? Are they dead? The questioner makes inquiries, and seems gullible to the offered answers. Were orators there, they would, perhaps, be less prone to distraction tactics. Insults sometimes hide a key, as the adjective does here – 'outspoken' contains a truth; someone fears the orators' capacity to *speak out*.

Cavafy described himself as a poet-historian: often writing, in great detail, about his own region with its wars, changing empires, migrations, colonisations, obliterations. Many of his poems refer to specific individuals. However, here, the tableau is vague: Where is the location? Who is the emperor? What is the era? Who are the awaited barbarians? No such details are specified, and – to a degree – it doesn't matter: the scene could be in many places, or many times. Cavafy himself, born in a Greek–Egyptian family in Alexandria under waning Turkish rule, fled to what was then named Constantinople in his late teens to escape a war. This war established the British as powers in Egypt, ousting the Turkish and French authorities. Cavafy returned to Alexandria after a few years in exile, and remained working there for the rest of his life until he died in 1933, aged seventy. His life was shaped by tectonic shifts in empire, colonialism, warmaking, enmity, treaties made and treaties broken. In 'Waiting for the Barbarians' the characters, setting and timing are more freelance than specific. So when is the poem set? Always. Who is in the poem? Everyone, everywhere. Where is it set? Here. There too. 'Waiting for the Barbarians' is not a fait accompli. Sardonic, ironic, satirical; the energy of the dialogue is toward exposure, rather than fatalism. Between the naïve – yet detailed – observations of the questioner and the spin-informed responses lies a possibility: if people keep asking questions based on the observed reality unfolding in front of their eyes, they might eventually believe something other than deceptive distraction tactics.

I've always assumed that the barbarians don't exist, that they were a ploy on behalf of the emperor, senator and other higher ranks to justify opulence, delay and control. The opulence is evident, and justified as satiation for the barbarians, who, while they do not care for 'eloquence and speeches' are apparently impressed by 'shiny, glistening emeralds' and 'expensive walking sticks / gilded and inlaid with silver'. To invent an enemy who'd only be gratified by splendour (yet would be bored by 'outspoken orators') is to justify indulgence without the possibility of accountability. When scrutiny is thus defamed, much has already been achieved. It's hard not to read this as a defence for freedom of the press.

The spectacle of waiting for a nebulous enemy means that the authorities can gather people in the agora, waste their time, foment uncertainty, delay decisions, explain ineffectual efficiency – 'Why has our emperor awoken so early' – justify mass disruption, and then blame the 'anxiousness and confusion' on tardy-yet-terrible barbarians, rather than have the whole charade revealed for what it is: leaders who are effective at organising the circumstances which only satisfy their indulgences.

> Why are the streets and squares emptying so rapidly
> and everyone returning to their homes so worried?

The drama doesn't reach a peak, it dissipates but does not diminish, finding a location in the worried hearts of 'everyone'. Revealed, then, is the other agenda in this spectacle: *look what we can do.* The citizens return to life in a new normal, where leaders can display power and control with impunity.

The barbarians play a convenient role. It's interesting that the word itself is tied to language. Common in certain Greek usage to refer to a strange or threatening foreigner, with less refined customs, it may be that the word itself is onomatopoeic, the barr-barr being a mockery of non-Greek speech. Language, then, calls non-existent enemies into existence, to play a role of fraud in a theatre of deceit. Strangely, the questioner is actually capable of truth-seeing, no matter how hard the truth (you are being deceived) is to believe. Perhaps we have an orator in the making. The questioner's inquiries seek *knowledge*: 'Why?' The questioner has been convinced that the responder's explanations are accurate, and will yield information that will explain the disquiet. This is not the case.

I often wonder about the second speaker of 'Waiting for the Barbarians', the one responding to the questions. Are they gullible, I wonder, repeating everything that's handed down in the gossip mill and spin-doctoring of the powers? Or are they part of the spin, knowingly obfuscating evidence with evasion? Perhaps they're a fool. Perhaps they're malig-nant. Maybe they're a liberal, maybe a conservative. Maybe both. Maybe neither. Maybe frightened. Maybe reassured by their own pretence of knowledge. I am distracted by their character, motivation and sources – but that, too, is a fruit of circumvention. Whatever the motivation of the responder, the words they spout would seem, to me, to be best ignored.

Cavafy ends, 'They were a sort of solution for us'. That modifier – 'a sort of'– catches in the throat. It indicates something not quite right, not perfect. The awaited barbarians solved something, *kind of*. A poem of questions and answers leaves us, the reader, with questions of our own at its end: what will happen the next time such tactics are employed for the purpose of group control? What will the spin be? Who can be believed? What is really happening, and why? Who knows what? It seems to me that the poem's strange end contains not cynicism, but a desire for change, for new characters with new actions. A turn or, in short, a revolution.

Each origin story contains tools for creation and destruction. No story is perfect: every myth requires the ones who repeat it to find its edges and fractures. Without this critical function, how can we get better ones?

Flower Wars

Nico Amador

It started with a bang
(some say a snap).
Then a watery isthmus,
a primordial goo
lipping along
under a purple steam.
Then pods shaped
like violins, then fish
wishing themselves
bigger fins, feet.
Then pterodactyl,
then mammoth.
Then ice and more ice,
the long walk, the centuries
in the wilderness,
the zigzag wander.
Then a valley.
Then a lake.
Then the herd, the golden
grain, a maze
of aqueducts singing
their blue song.
Then a city bigger than Rome,
pyramids, a god
some people called
a hummingbird.

A hummingbird
cannot be a man
but man can learn
to love a hummingbird,
to go to war
for a hummingbird.
This bird was at war
with the world
and it ate its enemies
behind a curtain of roses,
and the grasshoppers
never said a word.

'It started with a bang'. What started with a bang? The war? No – everything. 'Flower Wars' may be the title, but Nico Amador begins at the beginning of the beginning, and even that 'bang' is debatable '(some say a snap)'. Two narrations about the start of everything, then, a deft move: in this casual parenthetical aside, we learn that there's more than one start to a story.

The scene changes to 'a watery isthmus' – a piece of land, like a natural narrow bridge connecting two larger bodies separated by water. Time is a device of control in the short lines of this first stanza: while we anticipate the war of the title, a world emerges and evolves through 'primordial goo' and 'purple steam' and pods, fish, pterodactyls, mammoths, 'ice and more ice' and 'centuries / in the wilderness'. The first stanza is cinematic: depicting something exploding, followed by emerging expanses of land, then strange plants popping and gestating, populations of beasts – including humans – practicing survival in a beautiful, but brutal, terrain.

Eventually, the broad-brushstroke world-making begins to narrow, to 'zigzag wander' toward a single valley. We see a 'maze / of aqueducts singing / their blue song' until eventually the reader's gaze is focused on a pyramided city whose god 'some people called / a hummingbird'. Again, amidst the lush landscapes and drama, I note the plural possibilities: it's only 'some' of the people, not all, who name this god so. If this is a creation myth then it's conscious of the side effects of its creation and doubles back to offer alternatives to make space, to sow doubt while making worlds.

If Mediterranean means the centre of the world, then this poem firmly de-centres. This destination city is not the Eternal City of Rome but a bigger one, Tenochtitlan, the fifteenth-century capital city of the Aztecs, now the site of modern-day Mexico City. During the Flower War era, the emperor Moctezuma reigned over a time of peace – or, it's wiser to say, a *kind* of peace. He had established equanimity by 'incorporating' – i.e. conquering – nearby populations, integrating them without consent into the Aztec Empire, so perhaps it's more accurate to say that during his reign, there was the cessation of local intergroup warfare. Peace is layered, too.

Nico Amador's 'Flower Wars' – also the title of his collection – sent me diving into history and biology. A locust is a trans-formed grasshopper: under particular conditions, certain grasshoppers transform physically, swarming, as locusts, in massive numbers. In the era of Moctezuma this unex-plainable phenomenon occurred, causing destruction and leading to the question of what, or who, caused this? Certitude plagues us and many of our creation stories found their genesis in attempts to explain the unexplainable. In the face of chaos, we seek order, and invent origin stories that make causation clear: often with gods who punish through natural disaster. Did the world begin with a bang or a snap? What's bridged by the isthmus? Is the insect a grasshopper or a locust? Is it a singular or a slew? Who or what can be blamed for this destruction? Enter the story.

To address the emergence of unexplainable destruction during Moctezuma's reign of relative peace, Flower Wars were proposed. These events did not concern petals, or stamens, or colour; they were death matches, performed with elegant and eviscerating pageantry, with strict rules and choreographed decorum. The warriors still died though; no flowers undo death. Rituals like this are designed – it's said – to appease the gods, to stop punishment. All theologies hide other agendas, so I wonder who benefitted, in the here-and-now, from those brutal dramas – liturgical solutions to cosmic conundrums can sometimes be a tactic to unmake a king, or conquer a community. Sometimes I wonder if practices like these – whether in centuries past or the self-destructive equivalents today – show our inability to live well with relative peace. In the end, Moctezuma's Flower Wars diminished the fighting populations of the region so dramatically that by the time the conquistadores arrived in the sixteenth century, local resistance and solidarity was weakened to the state of being ineffective.

While insects swarmed Tenochtitlan the inhabitants were making sacrifice to an airborne deity: the hummingbird was a god of war in the Aztec imagination. Why sacrifice to such a god, a 'hummingbird' that 'cannot be a man', but which men go to war for? These lines reveal how the narratives we use to make sense of the world can spawn other stories that damage us: differently, yes; but dangerously, also yes. The real issue was not a god who punished blameworthy people with crop-destroying minibeasts. Such stories are distractions, self-defeating, meaning-making evasions from the real threat: the primal desire for certitude. This is not local to one place; the conquistadores came with more (and worse) gods, other stories, terrible sacrifices. They had need of better mythologies, ones that would harness collaboration against European destroyers.

I met Nico once, at a poetry festival in Madrid. He integrates the energies of his life in his art: he's long campaigned for living wages, participated in anti-mass incarceration initiatives, and worked to address discrimination against trans and nonbinary passengers on public transport. His sharp interests – as an artist, a community organiser, an educator, and as a trans man – are demonstrated in the probing question underlying this poem: what is our addiction to narratives that weaken the very ties they're supposed to bind?

'Flower Wars' is not only about Tenochtitlan, or the Aztecs, or a particular time in history; it makes a bridge between times where the same story occurs and reoccurs. The grasshoppers – the final line is given to them – 'never said a word'. They are not the real threat. The real threat occurred behind a 'curtain of roses'. Nico Amador suggests we need better stories, ones that allow for ambiguity where it is needed, but crucially, ones that don't defeat the storytellers who are making the story up.

When a friend died, I kept waiting for him to show up in my dreams. All my other dead friends did this, but he stubbornly refused. I even attempted to influence my unconscious, calling him to mind before bed, hoping for one last conversation, even if it was just a farewell.

He never showed.

So I did the next best thing and invented the dream I needed, writing out what would have happened: how I'd have made him a cup of tea; how I'd have wondered how to tell him what happened; the sound of his laugh; his jokes; his questions. Where dreams failed, a poem helped.

[UNTITLED]
Michael Wasson

But before you live
you must remember every word
your mother never said.
As in here's the most perfect hole
to reach into
because what remains
is a space like the hands
you're beginning
to forget. Promise me
before you live
you'll remember the darkest
you'll have ever been
won't be holding steady
a cocked barrel in your mouth
the wheat field below the house lit
by another autumn. It was always me blooming
you inside me. Before living
swear to me you'll forget
the way a body carves out its own
season to lie down in.
To never forget the trees
lining the field before the sun
sets at last. Beyond are the torn ghosts
you are to always remember.
There is a voice that leaves
will always hold for you there.
& before you live
you must remember that night
is always falling somewhere

in the world. Someday autumn
could be just another hole
that winter empties into.
Remember me for this hunger
I brought you into. That your warm
body has never lived
without me.

With the square-bracketed negation of its title, Michael Wasson's '[UNTITLED]' gives the reader an indication of what might follow: a poem that struggles to title what it contains. It's a love poem that evokes the ghost-words of a gone mother. It is also akin to a lullaby sung by a man to himself, having returned from the brink of ending himself.

Who is speaking? The dead? Perhaps. It's also someone speaking to himself, saying what only he knows he needs to hear. It's a naming ceremony, a rite of passage to mark an entryway to life:

But before you live
you must remember every word
your mother never said.

What leads a person to speak to themselves in this fashion – 'before you live'? Is he coaxing himself from survival to flourishing? Mothering himself with language? Is he facing life after the death of a mother, or the near-death of himself? Maybe. Possibly. In a sense, the personal circumstances of the poet's life are not a necessary template, because the particularities are powerful enough to reach beyond the confines of an individual. Entire communities of readers are addressed: their griefs, survivals, dreams, experiences and longing will be stimulated by these powerful words. Reading and re-reading '[UNTITLED]' on a flight today, I forgot I was working on an essay and became engrossed in everything this unnamed work evoked in me. I stared out the window, unseeing, attending to what Michael Wasson's words prompted.

What follows the poem's first three lines is the voice of the mother; a character who is saying now what she 'never said': instruction, comfort, truth, recognition of her son's crisis, a crisis from which he is now emerging. Her voice is steady, assured, unafraid to name absence – her own – and unafraid, also, to name the void in which the poet finds himself. 'You complete me' makes a blockbuster memorable (in this case *Jerry Maguire*), but '[UNTITLED]' has other work to do: the voice of the mother affirms to her son that he is incomplete, plagued by a sense of limitation and inadequacy. Someone I know reminds me that reassurance is rarely reassuring. The mother's voice here attempts none. Instead, she makes a demand:

> Promise me
> before you live
> you'll remember the darkest
> you'll have ever been
> won't be holding steady
> a cocked barrel in your mouth

Perhaps it is easier to narrate such pain in the voice of someone who has crossed the threshold to death. To conjugate these lines in the first person – *in my mouth* – would be painful. It is an act of love and kindness to put the words in the mouth of another, someone who can narrate him back to himself. He becomes the 'you' of his mother's address, a witness, a person capable of listening to another. Poems utilise technique, of course, but the best ones communicate with clarity, not just cleverness. Amidst the many techniques of Wasson's poetry, I am moved – over and over – by how every demonstration of skill is, in his hands, a manifestation of essence, not just style.

It was a surprise to me that double entendre wasn't just for sexy jokes. Translating into English as 'twice heard', it refers to language that functions in more than one way. Of course most language operates on multiple planes at once, but double entendre formalises a word or phrase's plural potency to great effect. Taken as a single line, 'There is a voice that leaves' is almost like an admission from the mothervoice that she's departed. However, 'leaves' is not used as a verb, rather as a noun; the plural for 'leaf'. The empty space of the break allows the twin truths to be felt: a voice leaves, but that gone voice still speaks, and calls attention to that which grows:

> There is a voice that leaves
> will always hold for you there.

A son is instructed to locate himself – no matter how he feels – among growing things, a somatic experience in which burgeoning life may communicate with that in him which knows decay.

What do you need to have experienced in order to need this voice? It contains comfort without deception, instruction without promise, emptiness without abandonment. It is a call home, even though home has changed. It summons rebirth, now that an old life has passed, and it mandates continuance. No birth is easy; this one certainly isn't. I am moved by the vulnerability of despair, and despair's comfort.

No wonder it's '[UNTITLED]'. Reading it, I find myself at the grave of a friend, hearing his voice from the kind earth at the bottom of the hill near the home where I grew up. Dead as my friend may be, he speaks life to me.

There is news of war on the radio; someone is approaching an anniversary of unspeakable grief; someone else is staring at what seems like the worst tragedy. No wonder a poet turns to his loved mother for the language he needs. His collection's dedication, in Nimipuutímt and English, reads:

na'íicyawa
for my mother

an inscription that binds all the poems to her, not just this.

In '[UNTITLED]', we hear the mother utter yet another demand: 'swear to me you'll forget / the way a body carves out its own / season to lie down in.' Place and time are everywhere: a wheat field, autumn, trees, more fields, sun setting, leaves, autumn again and then winter. But the voice that's beyond life is calling a beloved son to spring, a 'hunger / I brought you into.' Her living-but-not-living voice is called into being, she speaks the necessary. She exists in language's memory, the remembered sound of when she addressed him as 'you': 'your warm / body has never lived / without me.' There's no sentimentality in the words, no empty promises of *I'll always watch over you*. Instead there are 'torn ghosts / you are to always remember.' This, then, is the task of the living: to live, to remember, to bear with, to bear up, to continue in love and strength supported by a voice of love and strength.

If you only had a single poem by which to read the life of the poet, what would become apparent? The task is one I learnt at college: read a text very closely, and be attentive to its every implication. Then read more about the source, before returning to the text. It's not the only way to read a poem, but it's not a bad way.

[won't you celebrate with me]
Lucille Clifton

won't you celebrate with me
what i have shaped into
a kind of life? i had no model.
born in babylon
both nonwhite and woman
what did i see to be except myself?
i made it up
here on this bridge between
starshine and clay,
my one hand holding tight
my other hand; come celebrate
with me that everyday
something has tried to kill me
and has failed.

The clarity of the brief sentences that make up Lucille Clifton's poem – one of her best known – is one of its most compelling features. Composed of short statements and questions (one of which is in the imperative), these fourteen lines do so many things: declare the truth; issue an invitation; proclaim survival. '[won't you celebrate with me]' – as it is often known – appears to us on a page that defines its own rules: no title, and everything in lowercase.

Reading this aloud, I hear myself speaking an 'i' while at the same time embodying the 'you' of the unknown address. The addressee is invited to a celebration, but of a kind that's defined by negation: the first question is asked in the negative 'won't you . . . ?' and the life that's being celebrated is 'a kind of life'. Already, the individual speaking has had to make what's necessary happen for themselves. Who is speaking? 'born in babylon' is where the information begins: a place of exile, a place of culture, a place where people were taken against their will and made to perform for the king. I think of the Hebrew Bible, I think of Rastafarianism. There's another possibility in the name of this ancient city, though: 'babylon' holds the word 'baby' – if that's intentional, then to whom is the word addressed? The self? If no one else calls you baby, then perhaps parenting yourself is part of what shaping 'a kind of life' means. This writer is 'nonwhite and woman': syllables of pride, identity and glory; syllables, too, that are statements of power.

The second question of the poem, having started with 'i had no model', then established details of birth, gender and race, ends with: 'what did i see to be except myself?' This is a voice that's experienced absence, and in the face of that, has both sought and found herself. Why were models lacking? And why were there no options but to be herself? Maybe this is a recasting of Walt Whitman's 'Song of Myself', except it is not written in the exultation of self-actualisation, but in the exile – that 'babylon' – of the self. We witness this self on the page now, in sixty-eight extraordinary words arranged over fourteen lines.

In the presence of absence – of role models, of a god – on a 'bridge between / starshine and clay', Clifton has 'made it up'; a phrase often associated with falsity, but here recast as creation and innovation. The speaker holds her own hand, making a community unto herself, and to this community she issues an invitation in a clause split across four brilliant linebreaks:

> come celebrate
> with me that everyday
> something has tried to kill me
> and has failed.

Another old trick from literary studies: summarise a poem in four words taken directly from the text, realising that your choice reveals as much – or more – about yourself than the poem. Today, I'd choose 'celebrate', 'everyday', 'kill' and 'failed'; tomorrow I might be drawn to different words. But how can you overlook the 'everyday' and 'kill' and 'failed'? These words, in plain, unadorned English, are anything but plain. The American ideal of being *self-made* in a *land of opportunities* is a big dream that may only work for a small population. Clifton's poem is an American poem, but one that reconstitutes the economic imagination inherent in much of the American Dream's unconscious.

Who is being addressed? Who is this 'you'? Is it the reader? Some share parts of the speaking voice's identity of being 'both nonwhite and woman'. Others will hear an echo of their own circumstances in 'what did I see to be except myself?' Still others will find kin in the need to have made something up because alternative voices were absent. And others will admit – or are, at least, invited to – that they've been part of the 'something [that] has tried to kill me' 'everyday'. A roving 'you', then. Reading the poem today, I see parts of myself in the loneliness of the circumstances, parts of myself in the empowered voice, and parts of myself in the aggressor. The radical invitation in '[won't you celebrate with me]' is to admit the multiplicities of self.

I'm still trying to read the poem as if the only things available to me about Lucille Clifton are contained within the words. Whitman is evoked in the voice of this self, and the European tradition of the sonnet is addressed as well – fourteen lines revolving and hinged on a turn. This, then, is a literary voice, employing and innovating a poetic tradition to speak to circumstance.

After watching online videos of Clifton proclaiming these words, her pauses, her breath and clarity of voice are imprinted on me. Born in 1936, she died in 2010, and lived a life of literature during that era. She knew poverty and recognition, eviction and accolade. While her poetry was wide-ranging in topic – from religion to rape to abortion and evil and violence; addressing politicians and poets – the shape of her work is often similar to this poem: short lines typically without capitalisation. She had six children in seven years and said that her style followed necessity. She was often short on time, so she often wrote short poems.

'[won't you celebrate with me]' invites others who have, whether by identity and circumstance, had a 'kind of life' similar to Lucille Clifton. Reginald Dwayne Betts, a contemporary poet, speaks about how, against prison regulations while serving a sentence, he typed this poem out over and over. In a *New York Times* article in 2019, he wrote: 'I didn't know then that mostly what I was doing when reading Clifton, more than when reading anyone else, was understanding myself.'

A dialectic is when two seemingly opposing things are true at the same time: 'it was bright all night' is an example (unless speaking about a lightbulb, or Greenland in summer). 'Arguments on the first date', too, might be an example of a dialectic (or at least a reason for refusing a second date). When binaries engage and entertain, dialectics stretch, allowing for the 'yes, and' of imagination, empathy, and – especially – complicity. I love poems that can do this. They look back, like a mirror, and ask questions about my own elasticity.

How It Will End
Denise Duhamel

We're walking on the boardwalk
but stop when we see a lifeguard and his girlfriend
fighting. We can't hear what they're saying,
but it is as good as a movie. We sit on a bench to find out
how it will end. I can tell by her body language
he's done something really bad. She stands at the bottom
of the ramp that leads to his hut. He tries to walk halfway down
to meet her, but she keeps signaling *don't come closer*.
My husband says, 'Boy, he's sure in for it,'
and I say, 'He deserves whatever's coming to him.'
My husband thinks the lifeguard's cheated, but I think
she's sick of him only working part time
or maybe he forgot to put the rent in the mail.
The lifeguard tries to reach out
and she holds her hand like Diana Ross
when she performed 'Stop in the Name of Love.'
The red flag that slaps against his station means strong currents.
'She has to just get it out of her system,'
my husband laughs, but I'm not laughing.
I start to coach the girl to leave her no-good lifeguard,
but my husband predicts she'll never leave.
I'm angry at him for seeing glee in their situation
and say, 'That's your problem – you think every fight
is funny. You never take her seriously,' and he says,
'You never even give the guy a chance and you're always nagging,
so how can he tell the real issues from the nitpicking?'
and I say, 'She doesn't nitpick!' and he says, 'Oh really?
Maybe he should start recording her tirades,' and I say,
'Maybe he should help out more,' and he says,

'Maybe she should be more supportive,' and I say,
'Do you mean supportive or do you mean support him?'
and my husband says that he's doing the best he can,
that's he's a lifeguard for Christ's sake, and I say
that her job is much harder, that she's a waitress
who works nights carrying heavy trays and is hit on all the time
by creepy tourists and he just sits there most days napping
and listening to 'Power 96' and then ooh
he gets to be the big hero blowing his whistle
and running into the water to save beach bunnies who flatter him,
and my husband says it's not as though she's Miss Innocence
and what about the way she flirts, giving free refills
when her boss isn't looking or cutting extra large pieces of pie
to get bigger tips, oh no she wouldn't do that because she's a saint
and he's the devil, and I say, 'I don't know why you can't just admit
he's a jerk,' and my husband says, 'I don't know why you can't admit
she's a killjoy,' and then out of the blue the couple is making up.
The red flag flutters, then hangs limp.
She has her arms around his neck and is crying into his shoulder.
He whisks her up into his hut. We look around, but no one is watching us.

It is not easy to write a funny poem, much less a funny poem that is intelligent about argument. Denise Duhamel's 'How It Will End' works in such a way that its poetic skill and dexterity – not to mention its psychological insight – unfolds like a compelling and indicting drama.

The stage is the boardwalk. The characters come in twos: the lifeguard and his girlfriend; the speaker and her husband. So far so straightforward; two straight couples – one in an argument, the other observing it. Though observers can only see, but not hear, still 'it is as good as a movie'. What a simile. In a film, reality is suspended – people can fight, kill, shoot, change, die, rise from the dead, fly, and then moviegoers walk out afterwards discussing it on the level of entertainment. The characters are established easily: lifeguard and girlfriend work perfectly as archetypes, each a blank enough character that much can be attributed to them. The poet and her husband 'sit on a bench', watch without shame. As passive observers – they don't seek to intervene – they wait to find out 'How It Will End', the plotline and title of the poem.

The back and forth begins with playful and pleasurable projection: the poet and her partner are entertained, and mostly in agreement: 'Boy, he's sure in for it,' and 'He deserves whatever's coming to him.' Their only disagreement is over what the lifeguard's sin is: has he cheated? Has he not paid rent? It is when the girlfriend signals to her boyfriend – 'she holds her hand like Diana Ross' – that the observing couple begin to split: the husband thinks it's just a matter of the girlfriend needing to 'get it out of her system' but the poet begins to instruct.

It is at this point that the poem turns, both in content, but also form. Up until now the sentence-lengths have been a line, or two, or a little more; sentences with fifteen, or sixteen, or up to twenty-three words. But when the speaker states 'You never take her seriously' a long, 255-word sentence emerges, escalating and rising and demanding and accusing and identifying and assuming, building and building in a fight that everybody knows has nothing to do with either the lifeguard or the girlfriend. There are limited gendered roles everywhere, and underneath all of those, there is pain. Along with this drama is an almost wilful misunderstanding, and if the drama between the lifeguard and girlfriend had not resolved, the plotline would have continued. But then, 'out of the blue the couple is making up.'

What is this long sentence? It is impossible to state it without the pauses that – by Duhamel's insertion of discrete sentence packages like 'Maybe he should help out more' – allow for breath. Even so, it changes the tempo. Energy builds. Is it erotic energy? Is the argumentative energy meant to echo sex? If so, is it good sex? Angry sex? Is someone taking pleasure from this reenactment of complicated coupledom? Is it helpful? Are either of them satisfied? Has fighting replaced sex for the speaker and her spouse? Where is this going?

The energy dissipates as suddenly as the argument: the red flag that's hitherto been slapping 'against his station . . . flutters, then hangs limp.' If one hasn't been projecting sex into the unfolding lines already, then 'limp' brings at least one organ to mind. The lifeguard and the girlfriend disappear into the hut. The first couple look around, almost as if for someone else to project onto, some other tableau to perform the thing they can't bear about themselves.

One of the delights of this poem – and its subtle tease to an audience – is the usage of observation. A couple – the speaker and her husband – observe an arguing couple. At some point in the reading, we begin to pay less attention to the arguing couple and more attention to what's happening between speaker and spouse. It's been building, until the turn after '"That's your problem"', when the back and forth of dialogue escalates. Part of Duhamel's brilliant sleight of hand is that the reader is now involved. The drama ends with 'but no one is watching us' but that's not entirely true: the reader is watching the couple watching the couple. With whom do we side? Whose point of view do we discard, or empathise with? Do we like either of them? What of the reader is drawn into their drama, what does our connection with – or rejection of – either of them say about our own assumptions?

The conflicts between both couples are funny, hyperbolic, exaggerated in their gendered roles, insightful and infuriating. In such escalation, the temptation is to view the other through a tropeish lens of identity or behaviour. Every couple has conflict, and the question as to whether we expect the couple in the poem to survive is closely linked to our own relationship to conflict. That's the point. Who's watching? The lifeguard and the girlfriend seem to have found repair. Dramatic task complete, they quickly exit the scene, leaving the observing couple – and us the readers – with questions about survivability, arguments, capacities or incapacities to listen. Is repair possible? Or necessary? Do we think fault is split between them, or rests solely on one or the other? They are each looking for something that the other doesn't seem capable of giving. They know each other, they have routines – a boardwalk stroll for the purpose of people-watching: is this for enjoyment, or avoidance? How do we feel about what's happening between this couple? What does that reveal about our own lives? The couples' surface-level behaviour is just a caricature for my own more complex processing: they are acting like fools and also believably; they are each hurting each other while each is hurting; they are talking but not really.

Other poetic techniques lie hidden in the poem. There's repetition: the colours blue and red, that flag, and those three lines that each begin with 'Maybe'. Later, there are three more that repeat 'and . . . and . . . and', and shortly afterwards, two lines end with 'admit . . . admit'. What is the *maybe*, the *and*, the *admit*? Who is speaking to whom? What will happen with this couple? We do not know. The title – 'How It Will End' – with its conventional capitals, looms as an opportunity for the readers, and the dramas, dialectics and decisions of our own populated lives.

I've had a different relationship to the idea of 'resolution' as years have gone by, particularly in poetry. In early publishing, I ended poems with resolve. It could be deemed a rookie mistake, but if it is a mistake, it's nonetheless one that indicates disposition and desire. These days, I've changed my style: I write and like poems that don't necessarily offer soft landings, instead leaving the reader with some tension: the work asking for discussion, reflection and feeling from the one looking at the page.

One Tree

Philip Metres

They wanted to tear down the tulip tree, our neighbors, last year.
It throws a shadow over their vegetable patch, the only tree in our
backyard. We said no. Now they've hired someone to chainsaw an
arm – the crux on our side of the fence – and my wife, in tousled
hair and morning sweat, marches to stop the carnage, mid-limb.
It reminds her of her childhood home, a shady place to hide. She
recites her litany of no, returns. Minutes later, the neighbors emerge.
The worker points to our unblinded window. I want to say, *it's not
me*, slide out of view behind a wall of cupboards, ominous breakfast
table, steam of tea, our two young daughters now alone. I want no
trouble. Must I fight for my wife's desire for yellow blooms when
my neighbors' tomatoes will stunt and blight in shade? Always
the same story: two people, one tree, not enough land or light or
love. Like the baby brought to Solomon, someone must give. Dear
neighbor, it's not me. Bloom-shadowed, light-deprived, they lower
the chainsaw again.

Often it is the unexpected thing that starts it off. What's the *it*? Well, it can feel like everything. In this case, it's the tulip tree in the yard. The speaker of the poem is trying to describe the situation between 'us' (namely, a couple) and 'they' (their neighbours). The neighbours want to cut down a tree that keeps their vegetable patch in the shade. But the offending tree isn't in the neighbour's backyard, it's on the property of the speaker and his wife who loves the tree: 'It reminds her of her childhood home, a shady place to hide.'

A neighbourly drama threatens to unfold. However, as Philip Metres explores the underbelly of tensions in 'One Tree', a domestic drama is sparked too. The communications between the poet and his wife are put under strain and here, we hear the speaker's internal anxiety: 'I want to say, *it's not / me*, slide out of view behind a wall of cupboards.' He wants to escape.

And what about the tree? It is alive too, and is being cast as a character in conflict with the vegetable patch. Growing things against growing things. Shade where there should be sun.

'One Tree' is a prose poem. A prose poem can be understood in many ways, but in this context, I want to look at its shape. The borders to every side of the square are defined, apart from the last three words: 'the chainsaw again'. The poem presents itself as almost a clear block, like a property map with a little protrusion.

What is happening on this map? There is an argument about events occurring at the borders. Over near one of the frontiers of this square, a tree lives, thrives and provides shade: shade for a woman who finds comfort and reminiscence in its protection; shade to the vegetable patch on the adjoining property. Two types of shade: comfort and reminiscence for one party; the inhibition of sunlight for the vegetable patch. Chainsaw operators have been enlisted to saw off part of the tree and tension erupts between the spouses: 'Must I fight for my wife's desire for yellow blooms . . .'. The landscape of this small, squarish block of language becomes the story of the world: 'two people, one tree, not enough land or light or love'. The everyday experience becomes a window onto countries whose borderlands are disputed.

The speaker seems exhausted: 'Dear / neighbor, it's not me.' He is caught between a certain sympathy for 'when / my neighbor's tomatoes will stunt and blight in shade' and the bonds of love with his wife who remembers a tree as a 'shady place to hide'. The phrase *it's not me* has already occurred earlier in the poem – what is this repeated refrain? Avoidance? Certainly, or passing the buck: it's not me *but it is her*. Even the breakfast table has turned 'ominous' and the daughters of the household are 'now alone' in this great fear. The speaker worries that the tension will swallow him, so that rather than engage, he withdraws. This is in total contrast to his wife who 'in tousled / hair and morning sweat, marches to stop the carnage, mid-limb.' Their differing responses to the events reveals their inner conflict. Conflicts evolve, and what commenced it can sometimes be forgotten.

Is the real tension about a dispute with the neighbour? Yes, but not only – that's simply a catalyst. Is it the tree? Yes and no. The couple are united in their home and marriage, but within that unity lies the drama of how desire, response, pain and hope manifest.

Though the poem is about opposing needs, it is also about borders, division, and disputed territory; therefore its concern is also political. Philip Metres introduces a liquid alliterative list – 'land or light or love' – and declares that there's not enough of any of them. Is this true? Is that part of the ache of this poem, the hope that there could be more of what nurtures mutual flourishing? The tree has flowered and grown in land, with light, and has been a shade of love. The tree – the 'One Tree' of the title – holds story, memory, and love together. Could a vegetable patch be moved? Maybe. Perhaps not, depending on the size of the neighbour's garden. Is the compromise of an amputated limb an acceptable one? Maybe. Trees survive all kinds of modifications.

The poem creates tension amidst the archetypes evoked: the spouses who have vastly different responses to the neighbours; the children bewildered by the anger erupting between their parents; the poet who wants to resolve, or blame; the fate of the tree; the fate of the vegetables.

That 'baby brought to Solomon' is a reference to a story recounted in the Hebrew Bible wherein two people are arguing about the parentage of a baby. Solomon – reputed for his wisdom – suggests that the baby should be split in two in order to resolve the dispute. He knows that the true mother of the baby would sooner give up the child than allow such a thing to happen, and he awards custody accordingly. However, 'One Tree' ends without resolution. One of the acts of artistic restraint in Metres's work is that it doesn't propose a solution, even though it depicts a speaker clearly desperate for one. Those justified lines are interrupted in the final instance: 'the chainsaw again' evoking the question as to whether a machine that divides by brute force is the only option. The rest of the line is blank, like an invitation into the heart of the poem's tension, to imagine what the couples will do as they face a crisis that threatens to escalate.

Memory is a complicated thing – it's a sieve that catches some events, releases others; a cunning sieve, because some of what it catches might be recalled inaccurately, while other happenings are held with precision and still others are remembered with a bent more for insight than fact.

In the thousands of events that happened yesterday, why do I remember what I do: the early morning, those words that stung, the man in the blue coat with the rust-coloured scarf, the precise note the radio host's voice rung when she said *Really?* to the politician she was interviewing.

Artist

Vidyan Ravinthiran

When you were young you'd draw and paint.
Then your brother said all you could do
was copy down what was in front of you.
So you stopped. Sometimes you start again.
He's bought you watercolours. He is a saint
but what's done is done. I don't,
for more than a rearriving moment,
understand. For his role in your family was mine
in mine. How could I never learn,
till watching you, what sketching means:
touching with your eyes what has been given
again, and again, and again. It's the way you were raised.
The way you were erased. But I envy your line
that self-forgetful vigilance – its hesitation, even.

When I think of everything I've said to other people – siblings, friends, colleagues, strangers in waiting lounges, customer-service agents on the phone, customers buying items when I worked in a shop, patients waiting on trolleys when I was a cleaner in a hospital – it's overwhelming, and maybe at times embarrassing. Mostly, I am guessing that the majority of what we say to each other is not remembered. But some of it is.

Vidyan Ravinthiran's 'Artist' is a poem of profound intimacy about a moment in his wife's life: in her youth someone painted and drew; her brother made a comment 'all you could do / was copy down what was in front of you.' Now, years later, grown, married, she has shared this story with her husband, who has written a sonnet about it, holding the event to the light, examining it from different points of view. Every sonnet in Ravinthiran's collection *The Million-Petalled Flower of Being Here* addresses his wife, but the 'you' in 'Artist' expands the audience to anyone whose ambition to make is coupled with worry about their work's quality and originality.

The stage is laid with character – sister, brother. The scene moves from the past to the present, and the narratorial voice is generous. The incident is described without drama, and the brother's apology for his remark is evidenced in 'He's bought you watercolours', but nonetheless 'what's done is done' and the memory of the words has stayed.

Beneath the poem's action is a profound meditation on desire: the young person had a wish to be an artist, but was bruised by a remark: was it offhand? Was it intended? I don't know. A person with a passion is often the subject of comment from others. *It's just a joke* or *I didn't mean it*, we hear. But it's interesting how a pure desire often evokes dismantling attempts from those we are close to. The petty violence of the words that pass between us contains all kinds of intimacies and barbs. We know each other enough to say what might hurt; we are aghast when it does. We are secretly pleased for the cleverness of a quip but unprepared to learn how deep it cut.

The artist is talented and committed. She began 'young' and now – years later – sketches, 'touching with your eyes what has been given'. This drive – with its 'again, and again, and again' in a 'self-forgetful vigilance' – is nonetheless marked with 'hesitation'. What is this pause? Is it the awful question of *Am I a good enough artist?* or *Am I an artist at all?* or *Am I only copying?* It isn't always true, but it sometimes is, that the insults we remember best are the ones we suspect might be true. Is it possible that, while unkind, the brother's barb provided the motivation to keep going?

The artist has chosen a partner who holds a key, perhaps, to understanding something of the language of the past. Art calls to art – words and image married – each a method of paying attention. The blank space, the elegant questioning, the shifting point of view, the self-reflective analysis too ('For his role in your family was mine / in mine') demonstrates that both poet and painter are adept at questions of nuance, aware of the void that haunts creators, and the difficulty inherent in acknowledging your own gift.

The first eight lines of this sonnet follow a pattern of rhyme: ABBA, ABBA. The rhymes aren't perfect – 'paint' and 'again', 'saint' and 'mine'– but the emotional music of assonance is evidenced in 'do' and 'you', 'don't' and 'moment'. Then the pattern modifies: the ninth to fourteenth lines end with 'learn', 'means', 'given', 'raised', 'line' and 'even'. The words 'given' and 'even' echo each other's acoustic demands, the rhymes move internally: 'mine / in mine' 'again, and again, and again'. Two lines mimic each other almost completely: 'It's the way you were raised' is followed by 'The way you were erased.' In a poem about unforgotten language, the rhymes – formal and informal, end-line and internal – carry a poignant message: love, pain, memory, language, desire and drive are part of every life, and sometimes the smallest thing is a locus for life-shaping attention.

If I have the time (although this is rare) I like to write a poem out longhand. It helps me see what's there. Mostly, however, I type it. I noticed as I read back over my copy of 'Artist' that I'd made an error: 'When you were young you'd draw and pain' I wrote. The artist's vocation does include pain: the desire to excel usually comes with that ache of *What if it's not good enough?* or *What will others think?* (Good enough for what? A gallery? A textbook? Praise from a brother?) Technical prowess is what every artist might wish to improve. Even inspiration – that fleeting, strange thing – is temporary. But the impulse and propulsion to keep trying, to keep returning – 'So you stopped. Sometimes you start again' – is the sometimes-rewarding, sometimes-painful vocation of the artist.

A different poet, a different person, might have written about the bastard brother whose bruising wounds continue to this day. But the quiet action of Vidyan Ravinthiran's sonnet would have been failed by such drama. The brother isn't a devil; in fact 'He is a saint'. The technique of this sonnet does not require exaggeration, or conflate an offhand remark with trauma. It's intelligent about time, and intelligent about the way a person gives attention to that which they most fear. It sketches – with emotional sensitivity – how near to the heart our art is, how sensitively a person might wish to protect their making, and how closely we preserve the wounds that accompany our work.

In 1999 I needed help: I knew no way to navigate the complications of being gay in the form of religion I had soaked in; and I was drowning. I knew I needed help because a friend said to me, 'You're kind of fucked up lately'.

There was a flyer for a psychotherapy clinic on the notice board of the parish I frequented. I saw it multiple times a week. After six months of seeing the number, I phoned, and arranged a time. 'It's a big building,' the therapist said, 'so make sure to use the side door.' On the day, I was so nervous that I forgot the therapist's instruction and used the wrong door so I ended up lost in a strange building. A woman who worked there saw me. 'It's an easy mistake to make,' she said, 'I'll walk you there. Would you like a glass of water?' She must have seen me shaking and knew it was nice to have something to do with your hands when you're that frightened.

The kindest thing my friend did was to tell me I needed help. The second kindest thing she did was to let me find my own way.

The Drop Off
Molly Twomey

Everything's a blur. You don't play Talking Heads,
Bob Dylan, talk about work or your iffy stomach.

You read the road as if it's encrypted
with what a father should say on a drive like this.

Should I apologize for your missed appointments,
unread emails? There is always someone

who needs you more. Mostly I'm sorry
that I'm not as happy as you raised me to be.

I want to ask the GPS the quickest route to end this silence.
When we reach The Centre you pull up and go straight

for the boot. This is what you know to do,
to lift the heavy thing, tell me to take your good umbrella.

You drag my suitcase to the door where the nurse stands
with a notepad and clutches your arm.

I'll come back soon, you say,
but she smiles and says, *It's better if you don't.*

Occasionally I use a simple prompt when giving writing workshops: recall a single encounter where you said something important to a person. That's the first part of the exercise. The next part – equally important – is to ask 'what else was happening around you? What can you see? What were you doing with your hands? What was happening next door? Could you smell anything? Feel anything?' When workshop participants write their poem, they can only give the sentence exchange one single line: everything else has to be about the other things that were happening.

Once a fifteen-year-old student described an evening when she felt profoundly alone. Her sister, who was downstairs with her boyfriend, came into the room, and held her, and said something kind. The student described the green mohair of the cardigan her sister was wearing, the feel of that wool on her cheek. The sound of the boyfriend downstairs on the phone with his friend. As she laid her head on her sister's shoulder, she could see what was on the muted television in the corner. The single line she shared, the line of direct speech between her and her sister – I've forgotten it. I've not forgotten everything else though. I feel it.

Not every speaker of a poem is aligned with its author. Molly Twomey – whose surname is the English version of Ó Tuama, hence I feel like she's some class of cousin – has been public about how autobiographical her book *Raised Among*

Vultures is. Much of the collection concerns the time leading up to, and from, a stay in an inpatient facility for people with eating disorders. The book is like a long gaze: at the Ireland she grew up in; at herself; the excuses she had for her restrictions of food; the behaviours and anxieties of people around her. In form and music, she makes poetry out of precision. She examines her inner life, but also examines the world around her from the point of view of a patient.

Every encounter is linked to what else was sensed: what you were doing with your hands, what the weather was like, what was on the radio, a scent in the air, and the presence of the absence of certain things. Molly Twomey's 'The Drop Off' is rich in imagery, even though it begins with 'Everything's a blur.' The familiar music is not playing on the radio, the typical topics are not discussed: 'your iffy stomach' being too complicated a topic to discuss while driving a daughter to a clinic to treat an eating disorder. The father concentrates on the road, unsure of what to say, and the daughter wonders what apologies can bridge the gap between these two who seem so familiar with each other: Talking Heads, Bob Dylan, everyday parochial complaints. The humdrum of the ordinary, the relief and ease of it . . . it's all gone. They are in new territory.

Every time I read 'The Drop Off' I am struck anew about how this is less about the speaker and more about the driver. The dad is doing everything he can: driving, trying to find the topics that aren't too upsetting, trying not to say the wrong thing. His silences are silences of love. Awkward, yes – but love is often a little awkward when your world's collapsing. And what human connection hasn't at times been awkward? When they stop he goes to the boot of the car.

> This is what you know to do,
> to lift the heavy thing, tell me to take your good umbrella.

A poem has action, but here we see hidden action: the worry that you've failed, the worry that you're losing someone right in front of you; the worry that you don't know what to do; the need to have something to do with your hands. That suitcase is dragged – a verb from Old English that also carries the meaning of 'to protract'. The father is anxious to help but also reluctant – it's like he's losing a bit of himself.

The nurse knows: 'the nurse stands / with a notepad and clutches your arm.' She offers *him* the touch, and *him* the smile after he's given a promise of returning soon. 'The Drop Off' is about the one dropping off, not the one being dropped off. He's done everything he can, and it is his heartbreak now to realise he has no more to do.

That 'good umbrella'. I always return to it. Presumably he kept it in the car for his own use. But in a moment like this, his preferences don't matter. If his daughter is going to take a walk, he wants her to have some kind of buffer, some way of staying dry, some kind of protection from whatever the sky would rain down on her. The umbrella is a roof, a shelter, a cover. T.S. Eliot called items like this an 'objective correlative': an object that carries and conveys emotion. He coined the phrase while critiquing Shakespeare, saying that writing should place objects or sequences in such a way that demonstrates emotion, without the feeling having to rely on other poetic techniques.

Objective correlatives aren't just for literature. Someone who had regularly kicked me brutally when I was a child returned to my life when we both reached adulthood. It was difficult to know what to say to each other. They gave me a card – it was signed simply with their name – enclosing some money, with an instruction that it was to buy some nice shoes. We both knew what was meant.

Molly Twomey doesn't draw too much attention to the umbrella. However, her naming of it – that possessive pronoun 'your' and the adjective 'good' – add up to 'love', give the object an emotional weight that has sometimes brought me to tears. On such elegant syntax is art built. Handing his good umbrella to his daughter meant handing everything to her: whatever he had to give, he'd give. And the crisis of his love is that he can help most by realising that his work is done.

In a poem filled with the absence of words ('Should I apologize for your missed appointments, / unread emails?') and a soundtrack, it is notable that there are two iterations of direct speech. *'I'll come back soon'* the father says, and the nurse replies: *'It's better if you don't'*. The nurse knows human edges: a person at an edge realising they need help; the one who drives her there. The nurse stands at such an edge; notices the loneliness of the one who wants to do everything he can to help more, but must realise he can't. 'The Drop Off' depicts a moment in the life of someone seeking help, but also a moment in the life of someone who is learning new things about help.

Once, in a supermarket when I was seven – 1982, or 1983 – I was recounting a long-winded story to my mother. She was thirty-four, with four children, two more to come. She, presumably, was harried and rushed, and my (not very interesting) story pushed her to an edge. 'Pádraig,' she said, 'I. Couldn't. Give. A. Shit.'

My parents don't use strong language. Even still. So though I was only seven, I knew these words of my mother's were momentous. I was aghast that she'd used such language, and in awe that she could. Later that night, I told my older brother; me on the bottom bunk; he on the upper. He laughed himself to sleep.

I'm on the slope into fifty these years. I'm still telling long-winded stories. Hopefully to people who do give a shit.

Little Children
Caroline Bird

Politically they're puritans.
They gasp at nudity like it's 1912.
They're shocked by minor offences
such as chip stealing. 98% possess zero faith
in the concept of rehabilitation for adults.
As far as little children are concerned
forgivable mistakes occur before sixteen,
after that you're on your own. Their stance
against marital infidelity is Victorian and their
position on divorce aligns with the Vatican City.
Nuance is irrelevant to the infant moralist.
They sit in plastic umpire chairs at the dinner table
shouting out unintelligible scores. They're violent.
They'll head-bang a breast or stuff a sticky hand
up a skirt then just amble away
like raging misogynists. They won't even allow
their mothers to bring home a sexy stranger
on a Friday night. They disapprove of drugs
like Tory neighbours. Their standpoint on drunkenness
is predictably brutal, especially for women.
It's like the sixties never happened. They believe
every adult should be locked into a sexless yet eternal
marriage, never slip up or forget
even a lunchbox, and be completely transparent
and open to feedback 24/7. They're hypocrites.
They spy on you in the toilet. Parents aren't permitted
even the smallest private perversion yet a child
can secretly urinate in a drawer for three weeks
until the smell warrants investigation.

Their relentless indignation! Their fascist vision
of the perfect family! Little children are like
the tsarist autocracy of pre-revolution Russia.
Their soft hands have never known work.
Their reign is unearned.

On behalf of my younger self I apologise
to my parents for the simplistic, ill-informed
and ignorant questions I hurled concerning
their romantic and sexual life choices.
How could you do that to dad?
How could you do that to mum?
I was operating under a false consciousness,
responding to an imagined society governed
by laws I'd gleaned from picture books
about tigers coming to tea. I had no right.
No credibility. Imagine bellowing criticism
from the stalls after seeing two minutes of a play!
Imagine expecting universal loyalty whilst flinging
spaghetti hoops at the wall! Imagine having such
confidence in your innate philosophy of love!

We kneel to tie the laces of their unfeasibly tiny shoes.

The other week, I made a new acquaintance at a party. I enjoyed his company immensely and over the course of the conversation he mentioned his children. I asked which – between the five-year-old, the three-year-old and the other three-year-old – was the most opinionated. (I have the child-less luxury of finding opinionated children deliciously entertaining.) 'Oh God,' he said, and then offered me a three-year-old – the older of the twins – to keep. Forever.

We are all former children. There are some opinions I hold that I have held ever since I could remember; other opinions came later. I remember the outrage I felt when my viewpoint was disregarded on the basis that I was younger than the listener. Ludicrous. It fuelled a powerful rage. Now, though, of course, much of what appeared unreasonable to the younger me is perfectly rational, and what seemed like intolerable adult hypocrisy then has evolved into perfectly understandable adult hypocrisy now.

Caroline Bird's 'Little Children' – with its hyperbolic insight into the rages of adored and disapproving dictators – is as much a poem about adulthood than childhood. It is an adult voice speaking about the experience of being under the gaze of a politically attuned child. For the most part, in the brilliant opening stanza, it is the moral lives of parents that are being scrutinised: their naked bodies, their 'private perversion[s]', sex lives, marriages and divorces; the adult desire for autonomy; their recreational use of drugs or alcohol; their leadership in the family unit; their capacity or incapacity for change.

Children inhabit an adult world before they're grown, and are often accomplished observers of the adult condition. If the child is well cared for and happy, they are all the more likely to voice their conclusions with a confidence that is as accurate as it is inexperienced; all the while demanding affection, nurture and attention. The bodies – no, the lives – of their adults belong to them: 'they'll head-bang a breast or stuff a sticky hand / up a skirt then just amble away / like raging misogynists.'

Time and perspective are portrayed with elastic precision throughout both stanzas of 'Little Children', published in *The Air Year*, a collection released after Bird became a parent herself. A turn arrives with 'On behalf of my younger self', and we come to suspect that the child depicted was the poet herself, judging the judgmentalism of her own childhood self whose legal opinions were formed from picture books: 'I had no right. / No credibility.' The idea that a child's ideas need to be credible before being articulated is so ridiculous it's comedic. 'Imagine bellowing criticism / from the stalls after seeing two minutes of a play!'

Alongside amusing apology is an understanding that a child – if they are happy – should feel free to be a mini-dictator. When a child is lucky enough to have an 'innate philosophy of love' what else should they do but develop their confidence by hurling forth opinions as they decorate the wall with the food prepared for them by their long-suffering – if hypocritical – parents.

Staying with friends for a few weeks once, I asked their small son (three-and-a-quarter years old at the time, he informed me) if he'd had any dreams the night before. The boy assured me he had. With breakfast jam on his face, he recounted a story filled with monsters and dinosaurs. He cared little for accuracy, so I'm guessing he invented most of the dream's action on the spot. I have an interest in Jungian dream analysis, thus I wanted to explore further – so I asked 'And then?' The just-more-than-three-year-old continued the story of his dream, adding more drama. I repeated 'And then?' so the small boy, aware of my idiotic yet attentive audience, made every single answer about poop. The monsters pooped. The dinosaurs too. Everybody. Poop. Poop. Poop. It would have grown old quickly, but he was having so much fun that I was trapped by his dangerous combination of cuteness and humour. And that's my point: the word 'humour' (coming from the Latin ūmor, meaning liquid) originally referred to four bodily fluids: phlegm, blood and the two colours of bile, black and yellow. Moods were understood as an effect of these fluids (escalated nerves and high anxiety were considered a result of too much blood in the system, hence the practice of 'bleeding'). That much comedy relies on bodily functions belies this, and my friends' son is not unique in his humour, nor limited in his understanding of it.

Funny poems are serious business; as are moods, bodies and their fluids. The way that love can help you tolerate what would otherwise be intolerable is the stuff of survival.

Parents aren't permitted
even the smallest private perversion yet a child
can secretly urinate in a drawer for three weeks
until the smell warrants investigation.
Their relentless indignation!

Such experiences are manageable, somehow, with a sense of time, humour and age, alongside adult-escapist behaviours. Nobody would expect – or want – their child to speak with the solemnity of a politician: their task is to coat their faces and walls with spaghetti hoops. Love isn't easy, though – while few parents expect their children to understand the complexity of their 'romantic and sexual life choices', they may still wish for approval. Children's disdain for their parents' choices can be the stuff of heartache. Alongside heartache, the everyday understanding that is one of the tasks of parenting. I am sure that apologies help, but I'm guessing – in most cases – pardon is already granted. Pardon, from *pardonner*: to give, and give and give, to go beyond giving.

'We kneel to tie the laces of their unfeasibly tiny shoes' finishes the poem. To kneel: an act of obeisance to these small and lovable dictators. The adults love the wearers of tiny shoes even if they have to withstand a barrage of opinions about their failings. Love and presumption, service and withstanding, temperance and tempers: they're all bound together, held with the patience of time and change. The 'We' in this final line is generous, speaking perhaps for all who care for children; it also includes the child who, in time, may kneel to tie the shoelaces of their own beloved 'Little Children'.

During one long anguished period of my teenagehood, I saw my father race into the kitchen, grab some bread and wolf it down with urgency. I knew immediately what was wrong: that rush of dizziness that comes with low blood sugar. I get it too from time to time and crave milk, peanuts, sugar, bread, anything to stave off the panic. Seeing my father's hunger and need undid me. I went to my room, and then left the house. I couldn't stand the possibility that his was a body that had hungers too, even though I knew that already. He turned eighty the other week, I'll text him later on today. I'm one of the lucky ones for whom time's been enough.

Those Winter Sundays
Robert Hayden

Sundays too my father got up early
and put his clothes on in the blueblack cold,
then with cracked hands that ached
from labor in the weekday weather made
banked fires blaze. No one ever thanked him.

I'd wake and hear the cold splintering, breaking.
When the rooms were warm, he'd call,
and slowly I would rise and dress,
fearing the chronic angers of that house,

Speaking indifferently to him,
who had driven out the cold
and polished my good shoes as well.
What did I know, what did I know
of love's austere and lonely offices?

Including the title, Robert Hayden's 'Those Winter Sundays' comes in at one hundred words: a century of words in a poem I always associate with time. How long does it take to look back on your childhood – especially a childhood 'fearing the chronic angers of that house' – with the perspective offered in this poem?

Robert Hayden was born in Detroit in the USA in 1913. His parents separated before he was born and he was subsequently fostered by neighbours: Sue Ellen Westerfield and William Hayden. It was not a household of harmony. It was a household of battles and beatings. His mother lived next door and he frequently was in the fray of jealousies and violence. Having enrolled at Detroit City College, he worked for the Federal Writers' Project before returning to studies at the English Department at the University of Michigan where he eventually became the first Black faculty member to work in that department. He taught at Fisk University in Tennessee from 1946 to 1969 before returning to teach at the University of Michigan from 1969 to 1980, the year of his death. In 1976 he was the first Black American to serve as Consultant in Poetry to the Library of Congress – a role now titled Poet Laureate. His was a life dedicated to poetry, as well as a life that bore the consequences of abandonment. 'Those Winter Sundays' is from his book *A Ballad of Remembrance*, published in 1962, which gained him a large national and international audience, in large part due to its winning of the Grand Prize for Poetry at the World Festival of Negro Arts in Senegal in 1966.

The title draws our attention to the specifics of time. Hayden is speaking about some specific Sundays, the Sundays of winter. *When* is he writing from? I always assume he's writing from the distance of years, maybe even after his father has died. From this vantage point – in middle age himself perhaps, able to appreciate the demands of love more fully, a parent himself now – he can look at what he was unable to bear when he was younger.

Is this a work of regret? 'What did I know, what did I know' has an air of something like self-castigation. Perhaps he's saying he *should* have known. So one answer is that yes, regret is a throughline: he was in a house where a version of love was shown but he didn't comprehend the great commitment of that love. The fires weren't just lit on 'Sundays' but were burning on 'Sundays too'. There is love in the labour of the flame, but also in the 'cracked hands that ached / from labor in the weekday weather'. Inside and outside the home, in times of work and in times off work, there were endless tasks. 'No one ever thanked him' – the older poet indicts his younger self. The speaker places a heavy burden of regret on himself, but – even if he does – I do not blame nor despise him for the poverty of returned love: I feel the ache of those 'chronic' angers like a physical blow. His childhood was, at times, brutal. In many ways, the strength of feeling is about inadequacy: the older poet feels like his response of love was wanting. But neither the flames nor the freeze could quell the anger of that house. No wonder he dwelt on these feelings for years.

It can be difficult to make adjectives work well in a poem, but Robert Hayden's descriptors are extraordinary: *Winter* functions as an adjective in the title, and the first stanza has four: the 'blueblack' cold, the 'cracked' hands, 'weekday' weather and 'banked' fires. For the next few lines, a boy wakes to sounds in a warmed house: fires splinter and break the cold; a man's voice calls. Hayden allows complicated descriptions to sit alongside each other: the modesty of 'good' shoes moves me every time. His language craft goes further in the final, double-adjectived line: 'austere and lonely offices'. Adjective comes from the Latin *adiciō*, meaning 'to attach', so it attaches itself to a word to give some texture, some qualification, some insight. An adverb is the same, except the descriptive word is attached to a verb, not a noun: 'slowly' the boy had risen and dressed, and 'indifferently' is how he described the conversation between a son and his father who'd 'driven out the cold.'

When I hear the self-recrimination of these lines, I wonder whether it would have been possible for these two characters to have communicated. Should that frightened boy have discerned what the man was communicating by his early hours, his sore, tired hands rising flames? The father's love comes in a language of service, dependability, and provision. The son, though, is afraid. Fear is a language – alongside anger – that seeks safety and reassurance. To use Hayden's metaphor of flames, there are fires that warm and fires that harm. Fearing the latter, the poet finds it hard to appreciate the former. I don't blame him, even though he, at whatever age he is now, seems to.

The final word in the poem – offices – returns us to that word's original meaning: a function. To officiate retains the meaning in modern parlance, and office means role as well as room. Love's offices are lonely, Hayden tells us, and it can take time to grow into the workings of love. Austere, too – a word from Greek having a hint of a dry tongue. The father's actions were like kindling: for the fires the boy needed to burn in order to keep himself warm in a place of cold anger. Now that he's done that, he looks at the source of the warmth, and offers a poem of the most extraordinary compassion.

Love isn't always easy to give or take. And it comes in broken packages. How do we know what's enough, what's worthy of praise, what's not enough, what's acceptable, what's not? Time helps, we hope. And change helps too. It's hard to know if there was enough time between the speaker of the poem and his father. There seems to be a way in which 'Those Winter Sundays' is – finally – bearing witness to what could not previously be borne. It speaks to the integrity of Robert Hayden's imagination: I imagine he kept mulling over this untranslatable language of love as years went by. There's a long search for self-forgiveness here, as well as desire to declare a truth previously unacknowledged. More than one thing can be true at once, even in houses in which the hearts are not warmed with love for each other. This is a difficult truth to hold. It is also an important truth to hold. It might help save us a little.

There's a line in the Christian New Testament that's always moved me: 'I do not do the good I wish; instead, the evil I do not wish, this I do.' I remember reading this as a bewildered fifteen-year-old and feeling a connection across centuries: the time between the composition of this letter and my own time; but also the fact that an adult had written about such ambivalences – I assumed I'd grow out of such patterns of resistance.

Good writing makes connections between the aloneness of the writer and the aloneness of the reader. And that, strangely, can be enough. While some of us go to books for advice on how to change our lives, sometimes it's the familiar patterns of human experience – across cultures, across time – that can be a guide.

My Worries Have Worries

Laura Villareal

so I built little matchstick houses
with large ceilings, a garden for them to grow

tomatoes, cilantro, & carrots
their worry babies will eat

but they chew on the henbit of me anyway
both my past & future entwined into disasters

I tell them I worry about their health
that they're not eating properly

I mother them
the way I do anyone I love

they ask if I love myself
I tug the sleeves of my sweater

begin thatching a leaking roof
water their garden
at night

I can hear them
dancing around a bonfire

all I've built burned
down, a soot snowfall

tomorrow they'll wait for me
& I'll reconstruct their home
anyone would do the same

Does Laura Villareal have hope for change? It's hard to tell from the magical realism of 'My Worries Have Worries'; magical because she's turned her worries into independent, wicked, mischievous, compelling creatures; real because we all know how truly difficult it is to break out of a cycle.

The speaker is alone: 'I built little matchstick houses' and 'my past & future entwined into disaster'; 'I worry about their health' and 'I mother them'. 'I can hear them', she says, as they destroy the protection she's established for them: 'all I've built burned down'. Even then, even after the worries have torn down what she has erected, there is no turning to other people; instead the speaker remains tied to this most self-giving, self-destructive concern: 'I'll reconstruct their home'.

The magic is the characterisation. The real is the isolation. Where are the friends? Where are the phone calls? Where are the moments when life – work, the news, demands of study, deadlines – take a person outside of their self-contained whirlwind? The tableau of isolation is tragic and also utterly believable. It took me many reads before I began to wonder about the actual human company, the actual *lacking* human company in this poem. I do not believe this speaker has zero friends, or bad ones, but I do believe they feel alone. Worry can send us into ourselves: these couplets and tercets are predicated upon a drama that traps the attention of a person in an audience of one.

Isolation isolates, even though it's close to a universal experience. And we give much of our intimate attention to that which is parasitic: drawing energy from our energy, depleting our capacity to look toward what might actually nurture.

It's interesting that the materials for these worry-homes of Laura Villareal's are both flimsy and conflagratory: matchsticks. Her little worry-beings are the arsonists of her construction, setting fire to the containers she provides for them. Yet the construction of their buildings with matches implies that she, too, wishes to set something alight. For years, I've taken delight in the scent and sound of matchsticks going up in flames. The flare. The suddenness. What is to stop her burning that which burns her? Herself, it seems.

I mother them
the way I do anyone I love

they ask if I love myself
I tug the sleeves of my sweater

The worries are not the real worry; the real concern is the relationship with them. They are loved. Without them, what would happen? When they are unhoused, 'I'll reconstruct their home'. She justifies this pathology by projecting dependence onto little beings that clearly hate her: 'they'll wait for me'. She then universalises: 'anyone would do the same'. Here, even the 'I' is absent, as if the speaker knows how passive speech is often a place to hide a bomb.

I read 'My Worries Have Worries' as the attempt to employ art for the purposes of self-reflection; to externalise a drama in the hope that the drama can find its completion. As we have it, the end – defeated, appealing to the 'anyone' of everyone – is not an end. There's insight in this unresolved final stanza. We are left with ache: *I am trying to change, and I don't know how.* I admire the poem's use of art, humour, exaggeration, drama and hyperbole.

Hidden in the theatre of the relationship between the worrier, her worries and her worries' worry-babies, other information is planted: wit, first of all, yes. But this is followed by horticultural information – 'garden', 'tomatoes, cilantro, & carrots'; the knowledge that henbit is a plant useful for holding soil together during winter storms; thatched roofs; watered gardens. The speaker is someone attuned to nurture: and, while capable of considering the nourishment of others, is neglecting to nurture herself. This is not a secret. This is known: hence the drama, hence the delight, hence the self-confrontation. The land is calling her to feed on what it provides.

The repeated 'I' of the poem seeks to distance itself from the things that demean and undermine the sense of self. It's not easy, and 'My Worries Have Worries' unfolds, not as a *culmination* of, but *during*, the drama of self-improvement. The poem is intelligent about time, namely because it describes an unsuccessful attempt that doesn't result in giving up. There will be other, more necessary dramas: between housemates, friends, spouses, family members. These relational tensions have the possibility of enlivening, sharpening, hurting, healing and thrilling their participants. These interpersonal exchanges await, and will benefit from the awareness, emerging here, that the whirlpool of self-destruction thrives on the attention it demands.

Villareal stages her work as an externalised example of

drama therapy: personifying elements of the self into distinct entities, thereby escalating the conflict in order to consider what change might be possible. It is perfectly clear that the worries cannot be trusted: they are progenitive, producing babies upon babies, destroying then renewing their own burnt populations. They'll eat anything: what grows, the 'henbit of me', as well as time 'my past & future'. They thrive on attention, and while they are insightful – 'they ask if I love myself' – they have no interest in their mothering other's self-improvement: they need places to live, places to burn, new places to live, fires to dance around, rituals to enact, sacrifices of time to consume, worried gods to wait for. Reading 'My Worries Have Worries' my deep pity and empathy are with the speaker. However, my respect is with the writer: a person clear about what needs to burn. The writer is aflame, not with rage, but with art: art that will heat, not harm.

Growing up is tumultuous enough without doing so in a place of political tension. And yet, imagining the state of the world, I imagine that the majority of us have come of age during strained circumstances.

What to do about this? A lot, of course. Organise, vote and change. But also, our art has something to say: not because it's a solution – I'm always cautious about saying what art is *for* – but because art may be a way of describing, framing and observing what it is we've lived through.

Your Grandmother's House

Colette Bryce

The Toby jugs on her mantelshelf
are like a row of punters sitting at the bar,
red-cheeked, ever the worse for wear. In a mirror,
the Ulster Television News
or Scene Around Six: the latest murders.
Her call, weak, from the top of the stairs

(where *is* he?) *Son are you there?*, the stairs
creaking, footfalls, one by one. She steadies herself
in the unlit hall, enters and yes, she could murder
a nice cup of tea. A booth like in the bar;
a black banquette. The lilac light of the news
enfolds you in its trance, casts glints like a mirror-

ball around the room. In the convex mirror
fixed like a porthole to the wall, you stare
from far away, re-scaled, and watch the news
of a missing child as she frisks the shelf
for the spectacles she might have left in the bar
for goodness sake, but no, sure here they are. A murder

inquiry is what they want but is it a murder?
Nobody knows, with no body and the case a mirror
of the case last year (the talk of the bar)
where the child had been cowering under the stairs
all the while. She sets her saucer on the shelf
and settles back to wait for the news

headlines to repeat again. Your new
uniform prickles skin as you browse the murder
mysteries huddled fatly on a single shelf
and wait for your father to enter this mirror-
life in which he's come to live, in a room upstairs,
and take his place at the booth he calls 'the breakfast bar'

and make some awkward conversation. A bar
of chocolate. A soft drink. He'll angle for news
of your sisters, brother . . . *How's your mother?* You'll stare
ahead and fidget, What do *you* think? The murder
story cross-fades into the sports results and the mirror
holds a stranger, or some other self

who stares back blank as the child in the murder.
At the breakfast bar, as you knew
you would, you shelve this scene and exit the mirror.

Re-reading Colette Bryce's 'Your Grandmother's House' aloud, I am struck – as I always am – by all she manages to weave together: everyday conversation about the north of Ireland; the local bar; her granny; her dad; the state of her parents' marriage; and the news about murders into the complex form of the sestina. It's an old form, popular in writing classes because it's easy to understand, but hard to do. Sestinas are composed of six six-line stanzas, followed by a three-line final stanza, an *envoi*, meaning a stanza shorter than the preceding ones. A sestina – the word comes from the Latin for 'six' – has a further formal demand. The final words of the first stanza (in this case 'shelf', 'bar', 'mirror', 'News', 'murders' and 'stairs') must be the final words in each of the subsequent six-line stanzas, although in a different order. Finally, those same six words must appear in the short last stanza, two to each of the three lines.

What's the effect of this feat of poetic prowess? There are many accomplishments, but today, I am drawn in to a sense of stricture and control: the everything of the everyday, the unordinariness of this ordinary all crammed into a form tighter than that new school uniform, squeezed into the banquette that her father calls 'the breakfast bar'. Discomfort is everywhere: the jugs on the shelf are like 'a row of punters sitting at the bar, / . . . ever the worse for wear', the hall is unlit, the mirror 'fixed like a porthole' doesn't look out but merely reflects what's in the room, and even the television provides no relief – 'the news / of a missing child.'

Colette Bryce grew up in Derry, a border city in the northwest of Ireland, with a long history of culture, music, and – more latterly – troubles. I call it a city, but Derry is one of those cities that's like a big village. People know people. 'Your Grandmother's House' depicts a scene where murder is easier to talk about than your parents' separation. And murder is not simply the stuff of mystery novels: thousands have died in ongoing conflict about British presence in Ireland, both before and after partial independence in 1921.

A poem seeks a shape, and a shape carries feeling: it can convey anything from levity to weight. The seven packed stanzas of 'Your Grandmother's House' combine poetic skill with the communication of how a form – a dwelling – can leave a character feeling imprisoned. Reading any poem, I seek to find a place within its unfolding drama, but here, I want to escape it. The final line – 'you shelve this scene and exit the mirror' – almost accuses me of complicity: my own desire to leave the dense space means I abandon the young person to their own convex reflection.

This sestina's main character doesn't speak for herself, but rather, is spoken to: the second-person singular 'you' gives the effect of prescription, inevitability, entrapment, and a heavy air of silence. If this 'you' were to speak for herself, what would she say? Maybe she wouldn't speak, maybe she'd shout. The claustrophobic form and content leave me feeling the agitation of the unfolding action; when I locate myself in this house, I feel like exploding.

I find it impossible to read this sestina without thinking

of it as part of a poetic conversation with Elizabeth Bishop's 'Sestina': both reference homes, grandmothers, children and kitchens. In 'Your Grandmother's House' Bryce takes this structure and modifies it. The chosen six words do not repeat perfectly: 'shelf' becomes 'herself', 'self' and 'shelve' whereas 'bar' remains consistent throughout. Mirror appears to remain consistent too, but twice – 'mirror- // ball' and 'mirror- / life' – is broken across a line or stanza break. 'Stairs' becomes 'stare' and 'upstairs' in other repetitions; and 'news' moves to 'new' and then 'knew'; with a silent k, an unpronounced plosive in the eye, not the mouth. The word 'murder' stays mostly the same, moving simply from singular to plural. However, despite this minor modification, the sense of the word is fluid: referring at turns to a violent killing, an inquiry, a metaphor, a book genre, a desire.

Action is everywhere in these thirty-nine lines: the Ulster Television News is on; a grandmother 'call[s] weak, from the top of the stairs'; a daughter sees her father in a new light and cringes as her father angles 'for news / of your sisters, brother . . . *How's your mother?*' Alcohol is firmly in the foreground and background – the sevenfold repetition of 'bar' anchors that word's implications in every stanza. Even the jugs on the shelf bring a pub to mind, as does the banquette seat in the kitchen. We wonder if this is why the parents have a new living arrangement. More action is found in death, or its threat: murder is in the news, the disappearance of a child prompts rumours of murder, even a hiding child was assumed to have been killed until the child was found to have been 'cowering under the stairs / all the while.' The grandmother might be able to '[set] her saucer on the shelf / and [settle] back to wait for the news' but what child could cope with this level of menace without cowering?

With such a story, it may have been tempting to choose six other words upon which to hang the skeleton of the sestina: separation, grandmother, escape, father, and so on. The grandmother of the title is everywhere, but the child is alone:

> the mirror
> holds a stranger, or some other self
>
> who stares back blank as the child in the murder.

Who is this 'other self'? The daughter, obscured by circumstance and shape? The father, seen in a new light back in his childhood home? My sympathies go to the one who has to wait for time to unfold: everyone but especially the one being spoken to. The voice does not comfort, simply narrates, in truth, what's going on: with feeling, not sympathy; with clarity, not solutions.

The final three lines – that *envoi* – depict a young person who is already practising the coping mechanisms of adults: 'you shelve this scene'. I admire her: what else could be done? She is learning – or at least trying – to bear what is unbearable: she is witnessing the new circumstances of her father; she is in the impossible role of envoy between family members; she is against a backdrop where adults have learnt to live with murder when murder is the opposite of living. No wonder Colette Bryce employed a form so tight to describe a suffocating scene; it's the perfect choice to describe a terrible situation. Here, art heightens tension and does not resolve it. Instead, this tension bears witness to the truth of how strained the circumstances were: a controlled form depicts how uncontrollable life was for a young person.

Years ago, I fancied myself a singer–songwriter. Mostly it was the poetry of the lyrics that interested me, and it took me months to come up with any kind of melody that I could work with. One evening, someone said 'When are you going to write a happy song, Pádraig?' It was with friends around a table – candles, plates, homemade bread, dark chocolate, the guitar being passed around, empty bottles of cheap red wine – and we all laughed. While I do enjoy being happy, I recognise that it isn't always easy to write about.

The Orange
Wendy Cope

At lunchtime I bought a huge orange –
The size of it made us all laugh.
I peeled it and shared it with Robert and Dave –
They got quarters and I had a half.

And that orange, it made me so happy,
As ordinary things often do
Just lately. The shopping. A walk in the park.
This is peace and contentment. It's new.

The rest of the day was quite easy.
I did all the jobs on my list
And enjoyed them and had some time over.
I love you. I'm glad I exist.

What is personal happiness? Before looking up a dictionary definition, or doing a search through the tunnels of etymology, I decided to consider my own definition – the fresh feeling of a breeze coming in off the sea; meals with friends; great sex; reading poetry at 6 a.m. – but they are all particular instances of happiness, rather than a definition of it. *Contentment with yourself* is what I came to as a temporary definition. Contentment makes me think of things having their place with each other. The dictionary tells me that the word happy may come from words meaning 'fortunate' or 'lucky'. The Irish word for happiness – áthas – implies success, or victory, as well as joy. There are other connotations implied too: sometimes 'happy' can imply something like 'grim satisfaction'.

Wendy Cope's short poem 'The Orange' is an exploration of the experience of happiness. In ninety-three words she unpeels an experience, looks at it, savouring an ordinary moment that holds deliciousness at its heart: for herself with her friends Robert and Dave, for where she's got to, for what she's living.

Why is the orange 'huge'? Partly it fills the beat-requirement for this rhythmic iambic poem – where an unstressed syllable is followed by a stressed one – but there are plenty of one-syllable adjectives she could have chosen. Presumably the orange is described as huge because it was that. But why buy the huge orange? The colour and size of it like a small sun, like a warm coloured lamp; the smell of its oils on your skin. An orange is a thing of pleasure. 'The size of it made us all laugh.' Reading these lines, we find ourselves surrounded by group laughter before knowing who's in the group; hearing their delight about a seemingly simple thing. The orange isn't trying to be funny, or make people happy. It's just being an orange.

Orange is one of the words in English that doesn't have many easy rhymes, although sporange is one. There's a mountain in Wales named Blorenge and there's an old video of Eminem on YouTube in which he casts aspersions on the idea that orange is difficult to rhyme. All of that said, it does require dexterity. And Cope's easy form could be a play on the uniqueness of the word in English. Certainly it's a play on other kinds of form: the opening stanza contains two couplets that mirror each other perfectly: a sentence broken into two lines, with an en dash – in between each. The second stanza modifies that entirely, however, with a sentence that carries on for three lines, followed by an abrupt end-stop sentence: 'The shopping.' It is followed by further short sentences: 'A walk in the park. / This is peace and·content-ment. It's new.' The music of the first stanza is modified in the second, all while the pentameter beat is maintained. What some may deem a simple form is animated with playful engagement of skill and modification.

Wendy Cope's poems are often much more serious than they seem, and this is a perfect illustration. Here, a person, in the middle of a day with a list of things to do, shares company, fruit and laughter with friends, feels a sense of contentment, and takes pleasure both in achievements and in having 'some time over'. There's simple love here; for friends, for oranges and for the self. It's the orange that holds happiness. She has shared a quarter each with Robert and Dave while keeping a half for herself. That half to symbolise a sense of generosity, something she's glad to give to – and accept for and from – herself. The orange is like a satisfied orb, and somehow, so is she, for now. It's the ordinariness of it, alongside with shopping and walks that offer contentment. However, this is not just a poem about a good day, but a sense of this day in relation to previous, uneasy ones: 'As ordinary things often do / Just lately.' Those two words – *just lately* – function as a marker of emotional time. How long has it taken to get to today? What is it like to know that what brought you contentment once may not always stay? I think of those two words again when I look at the final four words: 'I'm glad I exist.' On the face of it, it's a lovely sentence, following the words 'I love you' addressed to someone undefined, perhaps even herself. But being 'glad I exist' is a sentiment that can be hard won. To know the 'Just lately' of glad is to imply knowledge of its rhyming opposite: sad.

The lunchtime is a break from a day with things to do; enjoyable tasks, not onerous or too numerous. Despite the implications of times when the poet hasn't been so happy, there's a fluency of cheer in the detailing of the day.

I remember once taking a lunchtime walk during a time when I felt burdened. It was one of those walks I needed to take in order to get through the afternoon. I'd promised myself all morning that if I could just hold it together till lunch then I'd get some air, some space, some containment. As I got back to work, I passed my colleague Jimmy. Watching him walk – with a bounce, with light on his face, with a warm greeting as he passed by – made me wonder what story my own gait told. But there was something contagious about Jimmy's ambling too: I can still remember how his shoulders were, how the spring in his step made him a little taller. Was he in love? Had he received good news? Was this just a natural disposition? I don't know the answer, but for twenty years, I've remembered Jimmy's gait that day. I know I sometimes walk like this too.

The light touch of Wendy Cope's 'The Orange' reminds us that what brings happiness one day may not be the same the next. There is no formula, although certainly a day with friends, a shared lunch, completed tasks, a new romance, ease of heart and time left over is a fine recipe. The three stanzas are not anxious to define or preserve the blueprint indefinitely. No existential meaning has been uncovered. Rather, we are brought into a moment of an individual's bountiful experience of time, finally unburdened, and their changed relationship to the present. It is a poem of happiness made manifest – that day – in the generous shape of a 'huge orange'.

I never had an appreciation for abstract art until my friend Jenn told me that she'd been painting one day. She'd spent a free afternoon with a canvas, paint, scraps of paper, shards of broken pottery, and otherwise discardable items. *What is it?* her husband asked, as she showed the artwork – power and confidence and muscle and energy in the arrangement of line and form on the canvas – blushing with the trust and truth of this disclosure. *It's how I feel*, she said.

My Feelings
Nick Flynn

                       Maybe I
should be locked in a cage in the center of
the village, a sign

the judge ordered me to carve hung around
my neck

to warn the children of what will happen
if they feed their animals. Go ahead,

use a stick, push the bowl toward me –

if you come close enough I'll tell you
about the years I was faithful, how good

I felt about myself, though she rarely
touched me – by the end we were simply two

abandoned orphans who'd smelled each other
out. These were the years

I believed the body contained the soul, yet
even so I began to feel like

a monster – disgusting, somehow –
until the shadow inside me

became me. I want to say we
really tried but maybe it was simply

the first moment I could be with someone
& say nothing & know

the other understood, or close enough, not be
overcome by my ~~extravagant subterranean~~

~~desperate flimsy shameful crushing guarded~~
~~inappropriate dormant~~

~~backwoods forbidden closeted~~
~~broken limited insubstantial fucked-up wounded~~

~~invisible unspeakable meaningless delicate~~
~~uncontainable elemental filthy~~

~~shallow feral misguided~~
~~distant tethered painful tongue-tied~~

~~wayworn purple~~
~~all-encompassing epic god-given phantom oceanic~~

~~entitled formal flickering~~ feelings.

When someone roleplays a therapist, they often ask the other person *How do you feel? No, how do you really,* really *feel?* The exaggerated caricature points to a truth: we often need help with feelings, and one feeling can reveal another and another and another. Even attempts to put them into words often come up short. Nick Flynn's 'My Feelings', then, is a poem that points to what words cannot describe, represented brilliantly in forty-five erased words: now you see me, now you don't; true and not true; yes and no.

It's tempting to give immediate attention to the obscured language that makes up so much of the poem, but Nick Flynn displays feelings before he defines them. The opening action of this poem – depicting a speaker locked in a cage in a village centre, with a self-carved punishment plaque hung around his neck – is like a nightmare of exposure, blame and self-recrimination. The central character calls for punishment: 'Go ahead, // use a stick . . .' and, far from denying his wrongdoing, is compelled to confess: 'if you come close enough I'll tell you'. This disclosure feels part-desperation, part-humiliation; part-regret, part-resignation.

What's the regret about? That things didn't work out, couldn't work out, with a lover?

> I want to say we
> really tried but maybe it was simply
>
> the first moment I could be with someone
> & say nothing & know
>
> the other understood, or close enough

What I admire about this is how he describes what worked: they found a shared inhabiting of silence, something close – 'or close enough' – to mutual comprehension. This is not about a bad relationship that ended; it's about how a couple with a deep connection found themselves manifesting regression as their relationship unfolded. They became like 'orphans' – a word usually used for children, but the term 'adult orphan' is sometimes used to describe abandonment that haunts beyond childhood. Reading the lines, it's as if the speaker wants the reader to reject him, but respect his former lover.

The scenes move from the tableau of public humiliation to the discussion of a love affair, then to the long list of erased feelings. Three different registers: beginning with metaphorical visual furniture, progressing to recollection of a present haunted by a past and finishing with a list of adjectives – both playful and painful – that erases what the poem evokes. The transitions between these registers is managed with a lightness of touch that's barely perceptible, a skill Flynn employs in all his poetry. Reading his work is like beholding his dream while it occurs: image gives way to memory which then gives way to feeling. The shape of the poem on the page is like a painting, using emotion as the paint.

At the poem's beginning, we witness a man proposing his own punishment.

> Maybe I
> should be locked in a cage in the center of
> the village

The village, not *a* village. The simple usage of this definite article renders us all locals, as a spectacle of shame unfolds in our community. More questions arise: why the centre? What exactly is on that sign? And why did he fantasise that he'd be the one to carve it? Punishment is taken for granted, but who is the judge, and what was the crime? The end of 'the years [he] was faithful'? The end of the relationship? The inability to escape whatever it is that was pursuing him? He's a warning to children 'of what will happen / if they feed their animals.' They, too, might come in touch with their own hungers, perhaps, as he barbs and begs for a bowl. Interestingly, if the children get too close they are not bitten, or scratched, or otherwise infected. Instead, they're given a story: language as warning and protection. This is a dream in which seemingly opposite things are possible at once: the chaos and the cure.

Does the body contain the soul? Is the soul eternal? I remember writing essays on this when studying scholastic theology. I neither cared for, nor understood what I was writing: it was all so abstract. No such abstractions here as the question of soul and body is relegated to the past. And anyway, whatever he'd believed about the soul and the body has given way:

I began to feel like

a monster – disgusting, somehow –
until the shadow inside me

became me.

The soul-enlivened embodied self is now a shade of itself.
It isn't only the tableau of the dream where opposite things
cohabit in possibility, it's also here, where the monster has
feelings – and what feelings! – in forty-five erased words.

The erasure – with a strikethrough line – is fascinating.
When reading the poem aloud, should I articulate them?
Should they be in a quieter tone? Or a more chaotic one?
Should they feel dismissed, rushed through, or should the
voice enunciate them as if each is chewed over, then
replaced with one that is different, but equally discardable?
Poems are made, in many ways, by the negative space: the
blankness of the page, the inhalation of breath. But here,
self-refuting space contains both the presence and absence
of language, the lengths and limitation of it. The cross-out
line itself is a visual feature, not just a diacritic. Vocation
and de-vocation, undoing each other. World without end.
Amen.

I've placed the erased words in order a few times, trying
to find whether there are commonalities, sequences or cate-
gories: 'unspeakable', 'uncontainable' and 'tongue-tied'
could perhaps find company with each other; 'inappro-
priate', 'forbidden', 'fucked-up', 'wounded', 'filthy' and 'feral',
too. Others, certainly the way I am looking at them today,
seem like outliers: 'phantom', 'oceanic', 'god-given', 'epic',

'backwoods', 'delicate'. And it's hard to read 'formal' without considering it a nod to Emily Dickinson: 'After great pain, a formal feeling comes –' (ordered as 372 in Franklin's arrangement). Nick Flynn's random sequencing, the ways that some words echo others, the tumble and mania of it contains a brilliant combination of form and feeling. All these words describe how no word will do, in thrilling demonstrations of emotional frustration. This is language about feeling, but notably, also language about the feeling of feelings. The struck-out list of descriptors is a demonstration of how feeling sometimes escapes definition, and at the same time can be the strange navigation method by which creativity rises to the surface. While the dream behind the poem intrigues me – so much is indicated by the long gap preceding the opening two words of 'Maybe I' – 'My Feelings' is not only about an individual's emotions, it also conveys the artistic process: feeling trapped, warning people away, facing yourself, and then watching as language and its absence conjure meaning and power.

I usually read through the full work of a poet every year. Sometimes it takes longer, sometimes it's slower. Usually it's a poet with a significant volume of work published, often they're dead. It all started during one of the busiest years of my life. I was involved in conflict resolution, deep in a few cases that seemed to be going nowhere, but were consuming my time and imagination. I'd wake in the middle of the night and worry about the conflicts I was mediating.

Like most people in this kind of job, I was overworked and underpaid.

I realised I was giving my favourite hours – between 5 a.m. and 9 a.m. – almost completely over to people who often seemed resistant. I needed something more creative. I took up morning yoga, after which I'd read some Emily Dickinson for half an hour, and then edit my own poems for an hour or two until it was time to leave. I'd arrive at work feeling refreshed, like my mind had been electrified by what enlivened me, rather than what exhausted me. In retrospect it was the beginning of the end of direct conflict resolution work for me: I finished that profession once that job ended. Poetry in the morning – reading it and writing it – gave me the space to make a change.

My Therapist Wants to Know about My Relationship to Work

Tiana Clark

I hustle
        upstream.
I grasp.
          I grind.
I control & panic. Poke
balloons in my chest,
always popping there,
always my thoughts thump,
thump. I snooze – wake & go
boom. All day, like this I short
my breath. I scroll & scroll.
I see what you wrote – I like.
I heart. My thumb, so tired.
My head bent down, but not
in prayer, heavy from the looking.
I see your face, your phone-lit
faces. I tap your food, two times
for more hearts. I retweet.
I email: *yes* & *yes* & *yes*.
Then I cry & need to say: *no-no-no*.
Why does it take so long to reply?
I FOMO & shout. I read. I never
enough. New book. New post.
New ping. A new tab, then another.
Papers on the floor, scattered & stacked.
So many journals, unbroken white spines,
waiting. Did you hear that new new?
I start to text back. Ellipsis, then I forget.

I balk. I lazy the bed. I wallow when I write.
I truth when I lie. I throw a book
when a poem undoes me. I underline
Clifton: *today we are possible*. I start
from image. I begin with Phillis Wheatley.
I begin with Phillis Wheatley. I begin
with Phillis Wheatley reaching for coal.
I start with a napkin, receipt, or my hand.
I muscle memory. I stutter the page. I fail.
Hit delete – scratch out one more line. I sonnet,
then break form. I make tea, use two bags.
Rooibos again. I bathe now. Epsom salt.
No books or phone. Just water & the sound
of water filling, glory – be my buoyant body,
bowl of me. Yes, lavender, more bubbles
& bath bomb, of course some candles too.
All alone with Coltrane. My favorite, 'Naima',
for his wife, now for me, inside my own womb.
Again, I child back. I float. I sing. I simple
& humble. Eyes close. I low my voice,
was it a psalm? Don't know. But I stopped.

At school, even though I loved learning languages, I regularly felt inadequate. When faced with one of those *Indicate the subject, object, noun, gerund, and both the transitive and intransitive verbs in the following sentence* exam questions, I'd tense up. If the question had been *How do you feel about the sentence?* I could have written a delicious essay. Feelings weren't on the syllabus, however.

Adulthood has been realising that I don't have to pass exams, and that I can enjoy such technicalities without the stress that my future will be decided upon the accuracy of my answers under pressurised conditions.

I say this because I'm interested in the verbs in Tiana Clark's 'My Therapist Wants to Know About My Relationship to Work'. What are the verbs doing? *A verb is an action word*, I learnt as a child. Not a thing, a person, or a place. I've counted this poem's verbs just now and I can find forty-nine of them, though I am sure that I'll count them again at the end and only end up with forty-eight. Or fifty. Let's say almost fifty.

The opening verb is placed on a line by itself:

I hustle

Even though 'upstream' follows, the simple present tense of 'I hustle' is set apart and predicts what follows. Hustle means many things: to jostle, or push, or scam, or toss coins together. It's used for work: a hustler can be a sex worker; a side-hustle can be a job you have in addition to your main job. Self-employed people use hustle as a verb that speaks about the way you're always thinking of the next job (and the next and the next) after the current jobs end. 'I hustle', then, as the opening verb, is an indicator of time, of stress, of choice, of creativity.

The verbs that follow are almost all in the present simple tense: 'I grasp', 'I grind', 'I control', 'I poke', 'I snooze', but this choice is not just about the present moment. The sheer volume of the verbs (I just counted again, there are fifty now, no rounding up needed) give a sense of an overwhelmed present: from creativity to business to relaxation to planning to pleasure to lying to study to collapse. 'always my thoughts thump, / thump.' The cascade of verbs contributes to an emotional undertow that associates even pleasurable actions with frenzy; restless sleep: 'I snooze – wake & go / boom. All day, like this . . .'

I assume we are hearing the voice of a writer: 'I see what you wrote – I like' acts as an early indicator of a writer who is supportive of (and perhaps sometimes compares themselves to) other writers, or who is commenting on, and liking, social media posts. Later on, the pressure: 'I read. I never / enough. New book. New post.' The importance of hustling up work is matched with the anxiety of keeping up: 'Did you hear that new new?' Who has time for this? Also, not just the new new, but the past: Lucille Clifton, Phillis Wheatley.

In poetry rules have function, but one of their functions is to be deliberately broken: 'I sonnet, / then break form.' Tiana Clark breaks form with poetic structures, but also with verbs: 'I short / my breath', 'I FOMO' – turning the acronym for Fear of Missing Out into a verb – 'I never / enough', 'I truth when I lie', 'I child back', 'I simple / & humble'. The verbs are simple, literally and technically, and so is the strategy needed for coping with the hive of this poetic mind. Language crumbles so that even the declarative of 'New book. New post. / New ping. A new tab, then another' is filled with the presence of an absent conjugator: *who* is getting the new books, reading or writing the new posts, hearing the pings, opening the tabs, the other tabs? The speaker has lost themselves in the doing.

The only time a verb is conjugated in the past is the final three-word sentence: 'But I stopped.' 'I stopped' allows us to think of two versions of the poet in time: the one who stopped, and the one who is now commenting on the stopping. Relief. Resolve. Catching up with the self. The poet is in a bath: bubbles, lavender. The explosion of 'bomb' is made pleasant by the domesticating alliteration of 'bath bomb.' The frenzy of the writer's thoughts is diffused by an infusion of scents and sensuality, sound and sight: 'some candles too.' The pressure to keep in touch has seemed exhausting thus far, but this – ironically 'All alone with Coltrane' – is a kinder experience of solitude. Coltrane's marriage to the Naima of the song's title ended, perhaps because he'd grown into his art in ways he'd previously not considered. The speaker, too, is growing into new things, new verbs. The motion builds a sense of the speaker feeling overwhelmed:

I start . . . I forget.
I balk. I lazy the bed. I wallow when I write.
I truth when I lie. I throw . . .

Even when the 'I' is absent it's there: who scattered the papers on the floor? Who stacked them?

I just counted again. What was I thinking when I said there were fifty verbs? Does 'thump, / thump' count as a verb? And if so, is it one, or two? Or twenty? If I knew Tiana I could call her up, but even she is probably unsure about what the verbs are verbing. This latest count got me to seventy-eight. Let's call it a clean one hundred.

We arrive at music before we arrive at music. Before the Coltrane reference, Tiana Clark has repeated a line three times:

> I begin with Phillis Wheatley.
> I begin with Phillis Wheatley. I begin
> with Phillis Wheatley reaching for coal.

Wheatley – an eighteenth-century poet, kidnapped and enslaved from West Africa – used coal as well as chalk to write on walls, later becoming one of the best-known poets of eighteenth-century America. What's the effect of this melody of words in the repeated language? Strength. Knowledge of history. Writerly friends, living and dead. Recognition of power. Recognition of determination. Recognition of trying. Try again. Try more. Try try.

The therapist does not want to hear about the poet's work, but rather the poet's *relationship* to work; the crisis seems to be the vocation of surviving as a writer. If this is the writing life, why bother? Maybe she feels no choice: 'always my thoughts'. What are the verbs doing? As the poem nears its end, they veer toward calm: the pace slows as the panic reduces. There is exhaustion of performative participation in the lives of others:

I tap your food, two times
for more hearts. I retweet.
I email: *yes & yes & yes*.
Then I cry & need to say: *no-no-no*

but it is eased with tea, a bath, salt, and some wisdom: 'No
books or phone'. This is a speaker who is haunted and enliv-
ened by language. Even prayer is gone – 'My head bent
down, but not / in prayer, heavy'. What's needed is not an
idea, but an experience: 'was it a psalm? Don't know.' What's
needed is a solution for holding the same body that's over-
flowing with exhausting possibility. She finds it in a bath:

Just water & the sound
of water filling, glory – be my buoyant body,
bowl of me

There it is. A verb of imperative glory: *be*.

'Do you know Thomas Lux's poem "Refrigerator, 1957"?' my friend Ellen Bass once said to me. I was staying with her and her wife Janet in California, for a night. Her granddaughter was there too, as were five rebellious chicks who escaped occasionally and wandered about the house cheeping and chirping. I learnt to look underfoot so as not to squash a living thing.

I hadn't heard of the poem. Ellen and Janet looked at each other, and then – solemnly, easily, with light on their faces – they recited the entire thing. Where one would pause, trying to recollect the next line, the other would come in. Their love for the poem slid into their love for each other. The yearning in Thomas Lux's lines found home in the light between them, the delicious sound of words in mouths, and the shared project of language between them.

Refrigerator, 1957
Thomas Lux

More like a vault – you pull the handle out
and on the shelves: not a lot,
and what there is (a boiled potato
in a bag, a chicken carcass
under foil) looking dispirited,
drained, mugged. This is not
a place to go in hope or hunger.
But, just to the right of the middle
of the middle door shelf, on fire, a lit-from-within red,
heart red, sexual red, wet neon red,
shining red in their liquid, exotic,
aloof, slumming
in such company: a jar
of maraschino cherries. Three-quarters
full, fiery globes, like strippers
at a church social. Maraschino cherries, maraschino,
the only foreign word I knew. Not once
did I see these cherries employed: not
in a drink, nor on top
of a glob of ice cream,
or just pop one in your mouth. Not once.
The same jar there through an entire
childhood of dull dinners – bald meat,
pocked peas and, see above,
boiled potatoes. Maybe
they came over from the old country,
family heirlooms, or were status symbols
bought with a piece of the first paycheck
from a sweatshop,

which beat the pig farm in Bohemia,
handed down from my grandparents
to my parents
to be someday mine,
then my child's?
They were beautiful
and, if I never ate one,
it was because I knew it might be missed
or because I knew it would not be replaced
and because you do not eat
that which rips your heart with joy.

I am writing this on a winter's morning, in Cork, after a family gathering yesterday. I'm staying in my sister's house. It's early, it won't get light until half past eight, so I am relishing the quiet that deep dark brings. I often forget how far north Ireland is until summer nights when there's light in the sky past eleven, or January mornings like this where the dawn is so late.

I'm here because we had an eightieth birthday party for my father yesterday. I'm one of six siblings, and while some live locally, others are scattered. We all gathered yesterday: parents and children, the grandchildren, and the spouses of my siblings ('backup singers' my sister calls them). The party was lovely but not without some quiet strain: somebody had been in hospital this week for tests. Diagnoses and terrible internet searches were on the minds of the adults. There was a looking-around, in the hope that the next time we were all together, we'd *all* be together, in the hope that we wouldn't be looking at photos of this day, saying sentences that begin with *That was the last time when . . .*

I say all this because this morning, in this quiet house, reading Thomas Lux's 'Refrigerator, 1957', my eye was particularly drawn to the linebreaks towards the end of the piece:

they came over from the old country,
family heirlooms, or were status symbols

bought with a piece of the first paycheck
from a sweatshop,
which beat the pig farm in Bohemia,
handed down from my grandparents
to my parents
to be someday mine,
then my child's?
They were beautiful . . .

Look at those final words in each line: country, symbols, paycheck, sweatshop, Bohemia, grandparents, parents, mine, child's, beautiful. A poem about cherries, yes – and we'll get to those 'full, fiery globes' soon – but a poem, too, about family, circumstance, the past, finance, migration, hardship, memory, inheritance and the future. Yesterday's party has me thinking of where I am in this litany of place, time, generations, strangeness and imagination. 'They were beautiful . . .' Thomas Lux's line reads, right after those powerful breaks invoking offspring. He's talking about the cherries, of course, but also speaking about the proximate strangers we call family.

Cherries then, and refrigerators, 1957, and – importantly – a voice. Clearly written in reminiscence, the speaker of this poem is in touch with his younger self, a self in wonder, a self who knows that words like *terror* and *terrific* come from the same source. The sense of awe towards these 'shining red in their liquid, exotic, / aloof, slumming / in such company' maraschino cherries is proximate to devotion, with all its demands, threats and promises. The cherries hold luscious power and sexual energy. They stand against the background of a childhood spent looking at a fridge full of 'dispirited, / drained, mugged' food, a 'childhood of dull dinners', where joy was most experienced in the yearning for it, not the event of it.

What was so forbidden about these cherries? They seem like a new forbidden fruit. Sex and desire are present, of course – 'heart red, sexual red, wet neon red / shining red in their liquid' . . . 'like strippers / at a church social'. These balls of fire might represent an unknown past of parents from Bohemia, but they also contain the future of sex and exploration for the boy. Why did he not eat them? Because he'd have been seen, and because this was not a household of pleasure: all those 'nots' following each other:

> Not once
did I see these cherries employed: not
in a drink, nor on top
of a glob of ice cream,
or just pop one in your mouth. Not once.

He is exploratory, this speaker, but also pragmatic: 'I knew it might be missed'. There's something other than the fear of punishment if he were to consume the cherries. Enigmatic though the cherries are, the jar is an object that both holds and withholds pleasure. He wants them in his life, and this means he cannot consume them. 'I knew it would not be replaced / . . . you do not eat / that which rips your heart with joy.'

Thomas Lux was born in 1946, so the year of 1957 makes him eleven. His mother worked at Sears & Roebuck as a switchboard operator and his father was a milkman. He believed poems could be a source of pleasure and also a way to endure. His poetry is marked by an attentiveness to speech patterns that are at once recognisable and also potent.

'Refrigerator, 1957' deploys drama deliciously. Its time-markers provide setting and staging: from the date of the title to the slow narrative pace of 'just to the right of the middle / of the middle door shelf'. The slow-motion moment is contrasted with the easy spanning of years in 'Not once / . . . through an entire / childhood', and 'over from the old country'. The craft of time is contained in elegant transitions from the particular – the cherries – to what they signify.

Sometimes, reading 'Refrigerator, 1957', I hear an existential question at its heart. 'Maraschino cherries, maraschino, / the only foreign word I knew'. *Who am I?* is what I hear: am I foreign? Are we? Partly? Foreign to what? The eleven-year-old is discerning that there is more to life than just the single story you tell about it: your parents have had entire lives without you, and your grandparents without them. What life lies before the curious boy? *Who am I? Who will I be? Will I have cherries in my refrigerator when I'm old?*

I like the Lux parents: they sound hard-working, loving, people of provision. They have migrated, and had past lives that seemed distant to their son – if not themselves. Did they, too, look at the jar of maraschino cherries with such ache and longing? Or were they mystified by their peculiar child who thought about the ideas of things, rather than the use of them? I don't know, but I like how the proximity of the family constellation doesn't undo the fact of how strange we are to each other, even kin.

It's slightly lighter now. I hear nieces creeping outside my bedroom door. Whispers of *Do you think he's awake?* and

His light's on. I am forty years older than they: a foreign country to them, known, and not. When I got up to make a cup of tea, I looked inside the fridge my nieces see every day: vegetables, butter, hummus, a few bottles of beer, left-over slices of yesterday's cake.

Out for an evening with a group of friends, one of them mentioned an ex-lover. His new beau made a joke – partly funny, mostly insecure – about being an upgrade. But my friend simply said 'I had a great connection with my ex, and still do.' He spoke about his former partner with no guile, no unkindness, no immaturity.

I wasn't that long out as a gay man myself, I hadn't had any real relationships to speak of. Already, though, I'd become familiar with the lexicon for ex-lovers: sometimes snide, sometimes with hints, often with blame. Here, though, in offhand remarks from a friend, I heard and saw something better.

Thank You: For Not Letting Me Die
Richard Blanco

for Michael Kalamaris

For: the mellow moon of your face, breaking
the lonely smoke of that bar with the brilliance
of your simple *hello*. I gave your smile my name,
and you gave my eyes yours, and that was all
the eternity we needed to lean into each other.

For: that first night you took my body, laid me
on the luscious cloud of your satin duvet, made
me holy, an angel, guiltless at last, worthy of all
the blessings of those divine kisses of yours over
my chin and shoulders, at each of my fingertips.

For: those juicy lamb chops I'd never tasted until
you played chef for me the afternoon you spent
aproned, lavishing me with a seven-course dinner
in your one-bedroom apartment, more tantalized
yet by the spun-sugar love we made as dessert.

For: that weekend you gave me in New York to lose
ourselves in, believe our love would go on, long as
5th Avenue's glam, delectable as Dean & DeLuca's
macarons, unique as the rings we bought in SoHo,
our vows breezy as that picnic in Central Park.

For: playing Shirley Horn for me through shared
earbuds as we flew back home, listening as one to
her lyrics as if our own: *Isn't it a pity we never, ever*

met before. Lyrics to love the lyrics of us: *Let's forget*
the past, let's both agree that I'm for you, you're for me.

For: those thirty thousand miles in midair and
those three hours you held me in the wings
of your arms, letting the man I had never been
die gladly, letting me be reborn in the promise
of your every breath breathing new life into me.

For: the fountain at *our* park when you told me:
I can't love you this much any longer. Trickles turned
into tears then, but now I hear what you meant:
that your loving would've slowly killed the man
you gave life to. Thank you for not letting him die.

I love how Richard Blanco's 'Thank You: For Not Letting Me Die' is written *for Michael Kalamaris*. Who is this man of romance, tenderness, affection and eros? We know so much about him, even his full name. We also know that he perceives the complexities that come with love, and that he knows what it means to truly desire the flourishing of another. To state the very obvious, this is a love poem. But one that encompasses many phases of love: its start, sustenance and ending. It pairs eros with candour, and displays the wounds that maturity leaves, wounds that have turned to wisdom and reflection.

'Thank You: For Not Letting Me Die' takes an old story – *boy meets boy, boy falls in love with boy, one boy loves the other boy more, boy splits up from boy, bitter stories ensue* – and reframes it: man meets man; they fall in love; what happens then? Luscious language, to begin with: 'the lonely smoke of that bar' was interrupted by a 'simple *hello*', smiles were exchanged 'and that was all / the eternity we needed to lean into each other.' *And that was all* – a linebreak demonstrating that this love has lasted, albeit in another form. Lovemaking is a language for the body, not the line, but Richard Blanco's syntax for sex throughout is a pleasure in itself:

> laid me
> on the luscious cloud of your satin duvet, made

me holy, an angel, guiltless at last, worthy of all
the blessings of those divine kisses of yours over
my chin and shoulders, at each of my fingertips.

Who wouldn't want to be one of these lovers? The wicked
sensuality of the linebreak at 'laid me' sent me cackling with
laughter the first time I read this aloud, and then the eros
unfolds further: not galloping toward climax but unrushed,
taking its sweet time. The duvet, the sense of self and other
that good sex affirms, and the rich experience of one's own
body in lovemaking awakens every inch of skin to aliveness:
'those divine kisses . . . at each of my fingertips.' Followed
by food, afternoons of meals, site-specific locations – 'your
one-bedroomed apartment', trips to New York – memories
of more food, purchases, 'vows breezy as that picnic in
Central Park'. Even the journey home from a weekend away
is recounted with romance: earbuds shared: 'Lyrics to love
the lyrics of us' – the sense that something new is created
in the space between two people.

There's a breathlessness to the life of these two men, and
it's hard not to hope this love could have been a lasting one.

It *is* a lasting love, the poem evidences that, but poems
about it use many shapes. One of the shapes is the humble
colon. Meaning 'limb', a colon has two uses in poetry, one
as a simple mark to imply an important pause, and the
other to indicate that that which follows will be a complete
thought. A single sentence, in two sections. Here, I think
of a colon as drawing attention, like some small ritual for
marking gratitude for loving relationships that ended. I
don't see the colon in a lot of poetry, but here there are
twelve, as if the very ink of the page is communicating:
take a pause here before speaking, because what's

unfolding is important. And what's unfolding? Gratitude. Thank you: for: . . . for: . . . for: . . . for: . . .

Gratitude is the creative technology undergirding this work. It's easy when it's easy. But gratitude is possible – sometimes – even when it's not easy. Sometimes it takes time to feel gratitude, to discern it among other experiences. The refrain-like repetition of Blanco's 'thank you' sounds like a ritual. We have rituals for acknowledging the beginnings of relationships – repeated stories of 'how did you meet?' Some people ritualise the end of relationships too, whether good ones, or complicated ones, or too-early ones, or bad ones, or couldn't-leave-quick-enough ones. Here's another kind of relationship to add to the list of such liturgies where the time has been enough, and the gratitude is plentiful.

'Thank You: For Not Letting Me Die' is so intimate that it feels cold to reference 'the speaker'; so I'll take the risk of calling the speaker Richard. Richard's gratitude to a lover is abundant. He has been changed: 'letting the man I had never been / die gladly'. Something came about in the encounter between these men. Reading the poem, I find myself projecting onto the characters, assuming the relationship involves one man new to a gay relationship. Maybe this is why one loved the other in a way that needed to let him go: '*I can't love you this much any longer.*' Whatever the particulars, something ended between them, but still Blanco has written seven stanzas in praise of the life that emerged from – and since – their love: 'letting me be reborn in the promise / of your every breath breathing new life into me.'

The '*our*', in its plural pronoun and italicised font, emphasises the irreversibility of shared place, shared memory, shared love, shared courage, shared sharing.

When something ends, it can feel like a life has to be split, that memories are broken, and the small recollections are shattered. Not here though. 'For: the fountain at *our* park when you told me', the final stanza begins. These lovers have not remained with each other, but their past is held together by a shared pronoun.

'Thank You: For Not Letting Me Die' praises what happened in the intimate space between two lovers, who revealed themselves to the other, who gave their bodies to the other. Blanco discovered something 'guiltless at last', hungers satisfied, needs observed, and – as is depicted in the wisdom of the lover's words – future pathways were discerned, even diverging ones. The gratitude is paired with sobriety: notice the 'Die' in the title. Maybe the long ache of guilt was driving a man to choices that may have led to destruction, and this experience – limited in time but unlimited in riches – was one that showed him what love feels like.

How long before the final lines of this poem could make their way to a page? Years? Decades?

> now I hear what you meant:
> that your loving would've slowly killed the man
> you gave life to.

This is what leads me to think that the more experienced lover saw someone who needed to experience other relationships, wasn't in a time of life where promising a forever would unfold in a forever, where the deep love between them would need to take another form.

I feel like I've got two energies in me: the energy that leads me to build bridges of understanding; the energy that builds walls against those who've been cruel. At times I've been led by one more than the other. At other times I've tried to hold them both. Sometimes that's been fruitful, sometimes not. I used to think that meant I was a failure. Now I don't. It's where the poetry comes from.

Facts About the Moon

Dorianne Laux

The moon is backing away from us
an inch and a half each year. That means
if you're like me and were born
around fifty years ago the moon
was a full six feet closer to the earth.
What's a person supposed to do?
I feel the gray cloud of consternation
travel across my face. I begin thinking
about the moon-lit past, how if you go back
far enough you can imagine the breathtaking
hugeness of the moon, prehistoric
solar eclipses when the moon covered the sun
so completely there was no corona, only
a darkness we had no word for.
And future eclipses will look like this: the moon
a small black pupil in the eye of the sun.
But these are bald facts.
What bothers me most is that someday
the moon will spiral right out of orbit
and all land-based life will die.
The moon keeps the oceans from swallowing
the shores, keeps the electromagnetic fields
in check at the polar ends of the earth.
And please don't tell me
what I already know, that it won't happen
for a long time. I don't care. I'm afraid
of what will happen to the moon.
Forget us. We don't deserve the moon.
Maybe we once did but not now

after all we've done. These nights
I harbor a secret pity for the moon, rolling
around alone in space without
her milky planet, her only love, a mother
who's lost a child, a bad child,
a greedy child or maybe a grown boy
who's murdered and raped, a mother
can't help it, she loves that boy
anyway, and in spite of herself
she misses him, and if you sit beside her
on the padded hospital bench
outside the door to his room you can't not
take her hand, listen to her while she
weeps, telling you how sweet he was,
how blue his eyes, and you know she's only
romanticizing, that she's conveniently
forgotten the bruises and booze,
the stolen car, the day he ripped
the phones from the walls, and you want
to slap her back to sanity, remind her
of the truth: he was a leech, a fuckup,
a little shit, and you almost do
until she lifts her pale puffy face, her eyes
two craters, and then you can't help it
either, you know love when you see it,
you can feel its lunar strength, its brutal pull.

Compassion is often called upon in times when it's hard to call upon it. After all, it's easy to be nice when it's easy – not that compassion means *nice* – and it's straightforward to be good when doing good's uncomplicated. It's when things get murky, muddy, painful and tough that the practice of compassion becomes a discussion point.

Dorianne Laux's 'Facts About the Moon' magnifies the demands of love and forgiveness in conversation with the gradually modifying distance between the earth and the moon. If you're twenty-five, the moon's about three feet further away from the earth than it was when you were born; if you're 'around fifty' it's six feet. The poem begins by depicting incremental distances, but its final description is the 'brutal pull' a mother might still feel for a difficult son, despite the fact that he was 'a leech, a fuckup, / a little shit'. Is this a metaphor for the moon's relationship to the earth and its population that has so grievously wounded the planet? Or is the pull between us and our moon a metaphor for parenting? Yes, to both.

The moon's effect on the earth is fundamental: it 'keeps the oceans from swallowing / the shores, keeps the electro-magnetic fields / in check'. As it moves further from Earth, what will happen? '[A]ll land-based life will die.' Not soon, but eventually. The speaker dismisses the idea that the primary cause of concern is the human population: 'Forget us', she declares in the shortest sentence of the poem. Her concern is for the moon, that orbiting, watchful body we 'don't deserve'.

The moon is compared to an eye twice: thinking back to solar eclipses millennia ago, 'there was no corona'; the future is described where such events will only feature 'a small black pupil in the eye of the sun.' Later, it's the wayward son's 'blue . . . eyes' we hear of, and then the 'two craters' of eyes on the 'pale puffy face' of the mother who can't resist yet another attempt to draw near to her offspring. '[Y]ou know love when you see it' the speaker states, and we wonder again which direction the metaphor is going.

I occasionally read (or, it's more accurate to say *try* to read) introductory books about theoretical physics. The question of time interests me, as does the question of space. What is space? The very word implies emptiness, but even with my faulty reading, I know that it's not entirely empty: there are quantum powers, gravity and other energies we cannot see. 'Facts About the Moon' is also about the forces, love especially, that occur in the unoccupied space between bodies. I find it hard to read this long single-stanza work without imagining all those who stare into space – whether at a horizon, the stars, a planet, a flame, or a television – seeking to strengthen whatever it is that holds them. A poem, too, holds itself together by its position on the page, the chosen gaps it opens, the turns from topic and line, tempo and address.

I grew up hearing about the Man in the Moon but here, the lunar face is that of a woman. Two seemingly polar opposites are described: the moon as mother, mourning 'her milky planet, her only love', and that grown child who might even have 'murdered and raped'. To distance oneself from a family member who has committed such deeds is understandable, believable, necessary even, yet we hear that 'a mother / can't help it, she loves that boy / anyway'. This is not a prescription for what every parent should do: there are many shapes for love, and many ways to communicate hope while establishing safety for yourself. 'Facts About the Moon' names terror and rage: 'the bruises and booze, / the stolen car, the day he ripped / the phones from the walls'. Who wouldn't want to bring such a mother 'back to sanity, remind her / of the truth' by urging her to make more space between herself and that which hurts her? However, there's a pull that disrupts increasing distance – calling, rather, for attention to that which binds us, despite strain.

I feel tension when I read this, pairing my own voice with that of the speaker, who wishes for clarity, 'sanity', safety for whomever might have been subject to this kind of despair and heartache. Yet, I know the layers of intuition, pardon and belief that tear us apart and hold us together. I've sometimes been the one drawn in, other times I've been the one pushing away.

Dorianne Laux is no stranger to difficulty. Her poetry reveals familiarity with trauma and survival. A working-class poet, her focus on everyday, tangible matters has been steadfast throughout her work. 'Facts About the Moon' is no different. It voices the twin drives for an artistic life: steady description about what is; attention to that which might guide us toward our better selves. There is no shame in the depiction of complicated compassion; the speaker is pragmatic, wanting to assure the moon – or is it a mother – that more pain awaits. Between the two voices is space for everyone: love takes different shapes.

I loathe when people speak about 'The Universe' speaking to them. Substitute 'God' and it just sounds like religion that blames populations for the emptiness of the promises they've been led to trust. However, Laux is troubling my loathing. She's looking at gravitational pulls – strained, yes – and transitioning between narratives of planetary–lunar interdependence and human relations. People do terrible things. People need love. Love is courageous. Love is costly. The ties that bind us to someone are not easily undone, and a universe of loneliness exists alongside the orbits that hold us. 'Facts About the Moon' does not propose a solution to the crises that compassion arouses in us, rather, it simply describes: fact and energy, ink and space, adjective and verbal noun, that 'brutal pull'.

My father's cousin is the family historian. Adopted in the 1950s, she's the one who's sourced birth certificates going back generations. Poor people who lived and worked at the train stations of villages in Cork and Kerry, loading and unloading supplies and stock. These were impoverished people, struggling with occupation, and surviving where and how they could. To have access to the simple facts of their names, occupations, and life events – sometimes even their handwriting – is a powerful privilege.

To have this history is a treasure. For this history to be erased would be more than the removal of data. It would be more like an annihilation: a making-of-nothing where there was something.

Exodus

Victoria Redel

We came from somewhere.   Had a village, & then didn't.

*

Trees broke in wind. A river went dry. Men arrived. A gang. A mob.
More by night. Fires were set. Then rains pressed through a neighbor's
door. We salvaged. Spoon & shoe. But might have chosen better. We
knew the importance of bedding.

*

It's simple math:

The want   &   the want   &   the want.

*

Don't talk about one long list of sorry.

*

Let's go, we say standing still.

*

In my grandmother's trunk I found a boat. In my grandmother's trunk
I found a boat & a train. In my grandmother's trunk I found a boat,
a train, August wind, the river Prut, an uncle in prison, a book of
addresses, a box of faces.

*

Identity papers were stamped.   At some point:

our name twisted to local consonants.

*

Look at the box of faces.   Worry & dignity.   What to do with the careful
dress, the good suit, the unpeeled orange in an open hand?   In smudged
pencil, on the back of each face, names I don't recognize.   No one left to ask.

'Exodus' – the title of Victoria Redel's poem – is also the name of the second book of the Hebrew Bible. A departure, a way out, the English word comes from the Greek, meaning 'out of' and 'the way'. To experience exodus is to get out of the way, or – as is the case here – to be forced out of the way.

'It's simple math:' the third of eight strangely arranged stanzas declares, before announcing 'The want   &   the want   &   the want.' The visual gaps on the page, also registered as sonic gaps for the ear, suggest what is lost, but more importantly, what is irretrievable and unlanguagable. What does all of this add up to? This is not simple mathematics at all. Whose want is being favoured? And at what expense?

To study conflict is to study change, I learnt as a young conflict mediator. Violent conflict is a project of enforced change enacted without negotiation, consent, engagement, learning or dialogue . . . It is many other things too, but once force enters into the equation, everything previous to the violence feels irrelevant. 'We came from somewhere.   Had a village, & then didn't' the poem begins. Victoria Redel's family, as she explains in her book *Paradise*, comprises generation after generation where no child was born in the same country as their parents. They had to flee: Turkey, Romania, Russia, France, America. A history of flight unfolds describing the effect of pogrom, holocaust, survival, guilt and memory.

Change is everywhere: the 'somewhere' that wasn't; the

'Trees [that] broke', the men who arrived, the fires, the dried-out river, the salvaging. Even the mathematics. In the face of all this violence, enforced change due to antisemitism, no wonder the strange logic of the illogical *'Let's go, we say standing still.'*

Let's look at the 'want & the want & the want'. Whose want is being given space on the page? It's a horror for me as I read it, because I find that the page holds the want of those families who wanted to survive. And also, in those comfortless spaces, the murderous want that drove those who hated Jews, the destructive want that took precedence over the safety and lives of Jews all over Europe. 'Don't talk about one long list of sorry.' 'Exodus' is not an excuse or an explanation. It's not a project of forgiveness, either. It's an enumeration of the leftover, and what's leftover is little and horrific.

In this family of survival was a grandmother, who had a trunk, a grandmother who took a trunk on a boat. The sixth stanza unfolds like one of those cumulative children's songs: *one man went to mow, went to mow a meadow; one man and his dog went to mow a meadow.* However this is not about a man, or a meadow, or a dog. This is a trunk that came by boat, and in the trunk is a boat. Looking again, it contains a 'boat, a train'. And looking further, it holds 'a boat, / a train, August wind, the river Prut, an uncle in prison, a book of / addresses, a box of faces.' The list is unsatisfying, the faces cannot be identified, evoking the earlier line: 'Had a village, & then didn't.' To be deprived of a village is to narrate forced departure: then we're back to the trunk, packed with both belongings and belonging. Was the river Prut a means of employment, a source of sustenance, or a passage of escape?

The penultimate stanza is extraordinary for its small change of register. Up until this point, most of the stanzas of 'Exodus' include at least one instance of the active voice: 'We came'; 'We salvaged'; *Let's go*'; 'In my grandmother's trunk, I found'. Even the third stanza is active with its observation of 'It's simple math'. However, this second last stanza of thirteen words is conjugated in the passive voice: 'Identity papers were stamped' and 'our name twisted to local consonants.' Who stamped those papers? Who twisted those names? The verbs are free-floating, can be affixed to the roving faces of whomever it was that enacted dehumanisation, forced exile and linguistic integration, before further Exodus and Exodus and Exodus. To bear witness to a sentence that iterates 'Identity papers were stamped' is to also see the words 'identity' and 'stamped' on the same awful line: I think of the Holocaust's tattoos and numbers, how identity was reduced to classification.

Immediately, Redel moves from passive voice to an imperative: 'Look at the box of faces.   Worry & dignity.' We see the dress, the suit, the orange and an open hand, even the fact that someone – somewhere – thought to write the names of the soon-to-be-forgotten so they would, in all hope, be unforgotten in the future. But there is 'No one left to ask.' I find myself exploring how the poem's shape contains meaning: the stanzas separated by an asterisk, a word that means 'star'. Stars like ancestors shining light. Stars like the Star of David. Stars like a sign of belonging. The shape of the separator contains many meanings.

I sometimes look through a poem and excerpt all references that fall into a single linguistic category: in this case I read 'Exodus' and looked for words – whether pronouns or nouns – referencing a person or groups of people: 'We' and

'Men . . . A gang. A mob. More . . .'; 'a neighbour'; 'grand-mother'; 'uncle'; 'faces'. Finally 'No one'. The sequence's culmination in 'No one' is powerful. This is a work of art, a lament, a sonic and visual representation of the lost. It draws attention to where the possibility of attention was obliterated, through death camps, forced departure, and local erasure: 'our name twisted to local consonants.' I read it and am drawn into its economy of language and the way that the page's emptiness holds content that's characterised both by collection and abandonment.

Information written in 'smudged pencil' cannot be recognised, because the stories are gone. In the absence of stories, we have this, a poem that addresses – in a unique form of eight mostly sparse stanzas, each separated by a star-like shape – some of the ways the surviving bear witness to the irrecoverable. The unrememberable are honoured in unsentimental ways. The work of poetry is elevated to the task of bearing witness to that which has been lost.

Someone wrote to me once asking me if I could suggest a poem of comfort. This person told me that a very close friendship had just ended: I don't know why, they didn't tell me in their message. For whatever reason, it had ended, and someone had written to an Irishman who likes poetry asking if anyone else had written a poem that might offer comfort or an echo.

Friendship, an easy word, is a lifeblood. A good friend can be among the greatest loves of our lives. And when friendships change – gradually, or suddenly; because of circumstances, or betrayals; for vague or sharp reasons – the grief can be as life-altering as the friendship had been. I was moved that the person wrote asking if there was a poem that could, in its own way, hold this heartache. At the time, I didn't have a good suggestion. This poem, perhaps, is something of a response.

Poem
Langston Hughes

(To F.S.)

I loved my friend.
He went away from me.
There's nothing more to say.
The poem ends,
Soft as it began, –
I loved my friend.

One winter, I decided to read all the poems of Langston Hughes. It was a difficult winter for me. He was my companion every morning. When I think of him, I think of a table in my rented apartment on the Upper West Side of New York City. I think of a cramped room, a lit candle, a pot of tea, a habit of reading that helped me drag myself through lightless mornings.

It's another winter now, a year later, close to the solstice. I've been up since before the dawn looking at the dark through the window. Reading Langston Hughes this morning is a reminder of how time passes: some aches deepen, some lighten. When I first read the twenty-five words of 'Poem' I couldn't bear it. The ache in that simple poem felt so specific that I closed the book: 'friend' shouldn't rhyme with 'end'.

Langston Hughes included this poem in his first collection, *The Weary Blues*, published in 1926, when he was twenty-five. He'd moved to Harlem a few years previously, and while he travelled widely until his death in 1967, Harlem was always home. There have been many books about him, and most of them deal with how the line between his public and private life was taut. Taking 'Poem' into consideration: who is F.S.? What was their friendship? Was it a relationship? Was it Ferdinand Smith, a Jamaican merchant seaman of Hughes's acquaintance? They'd met in Harlem. If Langston were gay, why did he not speak more openly about it, given the proliferation of other Harlem Renaissance writers who were more open about their sexuality?

But there are other questions too, questions that are less about the individual poet, and more about the poem. Do we need to know? What would knowing the answers to these questions facilitate in the work of the poem? What would knowing the answers prevent? The dedication – To F.S. – is unknown in its purpose. Even if both men were gay, were they lovers? Privacy is a right too, and in a public life, exposure of the private is not a right that an audience can demand. The space between the single-word title and the twenty-five words of the poem is dedicated to initials, and also holds tension for the reader. It tells us something, the meaning of which we will not fathom fully. The art of the poem lies in that tension too.

Before the poem unfolds there's the single-word title. 'Poem'. It could be humility, this title, or it could also be something grander, something that says at the heart of a poem is loss. Langston Hughes was no stranger to loss: his parents moved to Mexico City from Missouri when he was a toddler, and he was raised by his grandmother for most of his childhood, before going back and forth between his parents in his teens. He had an artistic patron in his first Harlem decade, but that, too, ended. He was among the esteemed writers of the time, but was critiqued by some of his contemporaries – and subsequent writers – for the speediness of his publications and his sometimes-present-sometimes-not persona in his writing. 'The poem ends', the fourth line states, and while that's only a portion of the sentence, it's the full line, and every time I read it, I feel that the absence of love spelt – or at least felt like – the end of poetry. 'There's nothing more to say.'

This is an early poem of Hughes's. It's filled with such grief. There is no recrimination in the lines: the first and final lines being simple statements of love: 'I loved my friend.' Simple statement of love? Yes, but it's in the past tense too: 'loved.' So it's love and loss. The repetition feels like a plea, and the lines are self-conscious about this appeal, with the repeated statement of love and loss being introduced by 'Soft as it began, –' There's the past tense again.

How would such a poem be received? I find myself on both sides of the poem: hearing – and feeling – the heart-break from the writer; wondering about the distance – 'He went away from me' – of the addressee. What happened between these friends? Did someone die? Did something break? Do pleas work? Sometimes. Sometimes not. 'Poem' leaves us in the long ache of love's loss, and – whatever people's feelings about Langston Hughes's recalcitrance or self-protection about his private life – the words function as a canvas for any of us who have become estranged from someone we loved. Love's losses continue, even if love doesn't.

This essay is difficult for me to write. Not because I don't like the poem, but rather because the poem is so true. As I write, I think of a loss of the past year. This loss is mine, but not only mine: mine to feel, but not mine to broadcast. Whatever Hughes's privacy may have meant, right now it enlivens me with both acceptance and accountability: acceptance of grief's tides; accountability to keep private griefs from public comment. 'Poem' gives me strange strength as well: look at what's possible, and survivable.

It's still winter as I'm writing this. I'm still in New York: a different house though. Small, like everywhere, but with a lot more light. What is the benefit of writing a poem like this? It may never have been read by F.S. But it states something about the speaker: a man capable of love, of friendship, of bearing loss, of moving beyond accusation or retribution, of being able – in the midst of living grief – to state that which was most true about this ended friendship: love. That's a lonely love. It's a grounded one, too. He may have lost his friend, but he has not lost his capacity for love. 'The poem ends' may be a way of the short stanza recognising what is past, letting go, and letting the last word be 'friend'.

In bad moments, I believe fruitless things: that other people are the sum of their worst actions, and that I am too. I've never been a fan of the kind of self-talk that asserts how wonderful and brilliant I am – it's simply untrue. However, saying *I'm a damned fool* is hardly a helpful alternative. I like how a page of poetry can explore the multiple selves I am: the ones that fail and the ones that flourish, and create an enlivening spark between these truths.

trauma is not sacred

Kai Cheng Thom

violence is not special pain is not holy suffering does not make angels abuse defines no one you are more than the things that hurt you you are more than the people you have hurt do not make an altar to your woundedness do not make a fetish out of mine a body belongs to no one a memory is not made to be eaten does it titillate you to hear about assault if i told you my story would you swallow it whole if i confessed my sins would you feed me to the beasts to purge your own i will show you mine if you show me yours we have all seen the darkness now give us the dawn tell me about the joy you keep in the hollow spaces between your bones tell me again how you laughed when you realized that you were not wholly unloveable i'll tell you again how i cried when my best friend told me that i was not a bad person remember how we used to count the lines on our palms when we were little how we used to try to read the future for its gifts how we used to make lists of the things we would dream of when finally we were free i will make you a list of the things i am grateful for i will sing you a litany of reasons to be alive i want to know the songs you wake up for in the morning i want to marvel at the unbelievable graciousness of your being i know that i am capable of pouring love like lavender oil into your cupped palms there is forgiveness like honey pooled in the chambers of our hearts you are the thing i am most grateful for all bodies know how to heal themselves given enough time all demons carry a map of heaven in their scars beneath the skin of every history of trauma

there is a love poem waiting deep below

Kai Cheng Thom is a Toronto-based poet who trained and worked as a social worker and therapist before moving more full-time into a career in literature, coaching and speaking. The mostly cuboid shape of 'trauma is not sacred' makes the work appear like a letter, signed with 'there is a love poem waiting deep below'. It's part storytelling, part survival, part advice.

Literatures have always known that to say something is *not* also recognises the possibility that it *is*. The assertion that 'trauma is not sacred' is fuelled by the knowledge that many have believed the opposite: that trauma *is* sacred, that violence is special, holy, makes angels, that abuse defines a person, and that an individual is simply the sum of their wounds. What is the effect of this? Isolation, manifesting itself in a sense of abandonment even from your fellow survivors. Creativity suffers as does song, as does the freeing possibility of forgiveness. 'i want to marvel at the unbelievable graciousness / of your being', Kai Cheng Thom declares.

To whom is she speaking? I've thought about this many times since my first reading. A particular other? A general 'you'? A self? A sibling? A childhood friend? A reflection in the mirror? Reading it again, I still find myself caught. It could be any of those. Today, it's narrowed down to two for me: a self, or a particular other.

There is such intimacy in the lines

remember how we used to
count the lines on our palms when we were little how we
used to try to read
the future for its gifts how we used to make lists of the
things we would dream
of when finally we were free

The space between the 'you' and the 'i' and the 'we' creates a narrative of such specificity that I am imagining the addressee is someone with whom Thom has been in communication for all her life.

The address communicates a history of violence, pain, suffering and abuse. Given these facts, how to live? How to think of the self? 'trauma is not sacred', she titles the poem, and spiritual themes continue: 'pain is not holy', 'if i confessed my sins would you feed me to the beasts to / purge your own'. This is a voice that knows the promises and perils of religion. However it is also a voice that – 'given enough time' – has found its way into song. The song praises a 'litany of reasons to be alive' and 'love like lavender oil into / your cupped palms' together with 'forgiveness like honey pooled'. These lines remind me of the ecstatic, erotic poetry of the Hebrew Bible's Song of Songs. Here, in this block of a poem, is a voice that knows embodiment, touch, sensuality, care and how tending to the body is part of nurturing the mind. Undergirding the entire poem is the presence of love: being loved by a friend, finding a sense of love in oneself, being able – from the experience of being loved well – to share love broadly.

I want to believe this poem. I want to believe in the wisdom of it. I've survived enough to know it's true. But I also return enough to old patterns of self to know it's not easy to believe

I am not my worst actions. The first time I read 'trauma is not sacred' I was surprised at the simplicity of 'i'll tell you again how I cried when / my best friend told me that I was not a bad person'. Why would someone need such a message? Perhaps because they've believed in their own badness, or shown it, or acted in the intimate and painful ways friends can act with one another. The economy of forgiveness is a shared one here: receiving it from another, giving it to another, receiving and giving it to self, too. Truth is another economy and not just the convenience of easy truth, rather an exploration of sustaining ones. This is hard won. I read an interview with Kai Cheng Thom in which she noted that for her – growing up as a trans woman of colour – lying was a necessity for survival. I'm glad she survived. I'm aghast at what survivals demand of a person. I'm moved by the truth offered in her poetry and – from a world away in terms of experience – I can connect with the wisdom.

The absence of an antagonist is wise on at least two levels: removing attention from an aggressor is a way of separating self from the actions of a wrongdoer; it also is a refusal to see another person as the sum of their offences. Who has caused such trauma? They're not mentioned. A person. A group of people. A mindset. A population. Self, too. And friends. '[A]ll demons carry a map of heaven in their scars' might apply to sinners as well as those sinned against.

At no point does 'trauma is not sacred' deny wounds, pain, suffering or abuse. There's a stoicism in the speaking voice: terrible things happen, and the past cannot be undone. The wisdom of time in these words is that the present can be affected by a changed alliance between identity and pain. If the mathematical corollary implies that suffering = me, then me = suffering. Understandable as the parallel is, Thom wishes – with vigour and verve – to assert that such equations are limiting:

> all bodies know how to heal
> themselves given enough time

she says, and I pause each time I read 'given enough time'. What's enough? Enough time to feel as loving as this speaker feels; enough love for another, or self. There are foundational practices praised here: art, connection, storytelling, joy, laughter, communication, friendship, risk, reminiscence, survival, dreaming, singing, forgiveness, sensuality and survival. Enough of these help connect us with the 'love poem waiting deep below'.

A relative of mine died the day before he was due to turn fifty. I was thirty years younger, and when I told my boss that I needed a morning off for a funeral, she asked me about the man who'd died. 'Only fifty?' she said, 'my god, so young.' I pretended to agree, when in reality I thought fifty seemed a lifetime away.

I'll be fifty next year. Friends of mine – people in their twenties – sometimes express affectionate surprise if I happen to demonstrate proficiency at a skill they think belongs to the realm of youth. I don't mind; I know there are things you can only learn with time, such as how time feels as it's going by. I'm glad for a life in which, since I was young, I had friends who were far older than me, and now, nearing fifty, have beloved friends far younger.

Ordinary Sugar
Amanda Gunn

Aunt Mary made graham
cracker cake without
measuring cups, divided
one pound light
brown sugar with a knife,
half for the cake and half
for the pearlescent
hand-beaten, double-boiled
icing. Aunt Earline made
yellow cake with frosting
of real fudge – 234 degrees
and all, slow cooled, poured
just before the rapid and
irrevocable hardening.
Ordinary sugar coaxed
to its epiphany.

An heir to their confectionery
sleight of hand, I keep
their notes pressed in a book
and safe. Sugar is poison
to my arthritic knees,
but their recipes will rest,
nonetheless, pristine,
not spoiled with things that
just seem sweet. I'll make
savory dishes out of what
grows green, what snaps
pleasurably, what must,

after twice the loss
of such women, be plenty.

Of Grandma Mattie, sugar
alchemist, it is said, if they
were all she had to hand,
she could make sweet potato
pie out of russets. Seduce
their pale starches until they
tumbled into caramel.
What the loving living tell.
I remember her gleaming
glass eye, her pregnant
wordlessness, her spinning
through the kitchen hot
and fast. Too, the ruthless
manic canning, putting by,
putting by, against memories
too near starvation — the
machine in her belly built
to last. I do not have preserved
in my book how she seasoned
her pear chow-chow or trapped
the summer gardens her labors
made lush. I know only that
she fed the earth her eggshells
and morning coffee grounds,
that she harvested continually
and in fullness, the tender skins
near breaking, near sugar,
always before the chill. Not one
bite lost. She'd mastered,

in a life, how to grow
a winter meal, to till, to weed,
to water, to tend, learned how,
I hope, to be satisfied.

Help me, Lord, to be satisfied.
I was born impatient, under
a vibrating star. But my mother
taught me gently, before
it ached us both to stand,
how to slice fat into cold flour,
sprinkle ice water by tablespoons,
form a perfect discus of dough
without touching it. Unfurl
the crust from a good
French pin. Brush with milk.
A proper flute. Taught me,
too, how to discern and sort
and sugar down the fruit,
and when to fill the plate,
and when to wait, instead,
for the juice to come in.

Amanda Gunn's 'Ordinary Sugar' is a praise poem: of aunts, grandmothers, and mothers, of the self too; of sweet things in harsh years; of horticultural skill; of business; of pleasure. It begins informally, with 'Aunt Mary'. Not *My Aunt Mary*, or *Our Aunt Mary*; rather, we go straight to the familial, as if we're already part of the circle. The reader is meant to know who this woman is, and the hospitable presumption at the poem's opening allows for all that unfurls: family recipes, differences, skills and survivals, time and lore. Aunt Mary doesn't measure. She divides 'one pound light / brown sugar with a knife' (my kind of cook!). Aunt Earline, however, is precise: she brings sweet ingredients to 234 degrees to make real fudge. Both kept notes, which the speaker keeps 'pressed in a book / and safe'.

'Safe': every time I see that word, enjambed for emphasis, I think of how these handwritten messages keep a person safe, but are also like a safe, and are a way of making safety. No matter that sugar, now, is 'poison / to my arthritic knees', the preservation of these aunts' recipes is the stuff of nurture. Their skill is mixed into the skill of the niece-poet:

> what must,
> after twice the loss
> of such women, be plenty

In hearing of 'loss', we may be learning about the deaths of Mary and Earline, or some of the losses borne by this community of women. The notes are also a way their heir keeps the legacy and love of her aunts alive.

Grandma Mattie – again, she's our grandma in this poem too – is an 'alchemist' alloying sugars from unsuspected sources: finding the luscious in russets. Finding? No, seducing the sweet from savoury spuds until 'they / tumbled into caramel.' Mattie's silence is pregnant, but she's a woman in motion: even her glass eye gleams, as we see her 'spinning / through the kitchen hot / and fast.' Why such silence and such speed? Necessity, presumably: the need for canning, preserving, preventing repetitions of starvation. Perhaps it is her horticultural industriousness that kept her moving – the garden was a business for her – recycling eggshells and coffee grounds into the earth that she 'harvested continually'. 'Not one / bite lost' the poem tells us. Skill and survival wrapped into a life that knew how to survive all kinds of winters – and to nurture others in such winters too.

There is distance and distinction between the speaker of the poem and her women. The poison of sugar, yes. But also, perhaps, the death of the aunts, and the last lines of the long third stanza in which the grandmother 'learned how, / I hope, to be satisfied.' Were it to simply say *learned how to be satisfied* it'd work as a statement of fact, or opinion. But the 'I hope' gives modification and texture. Did the poet ever know Grandma Mattie, whose culinary magic, 'it is said,' was legendary? Did Mary and Earline pass on stories of Grandma Mattie the way that Gunn – 'What the loving living tell'– is passing on stories now? Distance and hardship. Winter and work. Survival and sugar. These things are bridged by taste, memory of sensual delight, flavours passed down through sweet anecdote. This is a poem about how hardship was ordinary and how these women worked sugar into it.

'Help me, Lord, to be satisfied.' The final stanza's form turns towards prayer, a kind of sigh, an address that may echo the addresses of many forebears. If speedy Grandma Mattie never managed to find satisfaction, then the grand-daughter wishes for it, despite being 'born impatient, under / a vibrating star.' I see the spinning of the grandmother mirrored in the pulsing star: winter meals prepared to nurture a life that could go beyond 'memories / too near starvation.'

There were six children in our family, and my father speaks of the years where the last week before the salary was a week without money. I never knew this, though: love comes in filled stomachs as well as language. There was home-made bread. And homemade jam. Nothing fancy. Spuds and peas and carrots and whatever meat might have been available. The first time I was in a restaurant – I think I was eighteen – I didn't know what to do, how to order. I don't know how my mother ran the business of keeping growing children growing, but she did. When there was chocolate, it didn't last long. There was always food, though. Gunn's praising of the skills of her matriarchs leads me to praise mine.

I don't, and won't, have any children. I notice that this poem looks back, without any reference to future genera-tions. Childbearing is one way of giving to the future; providing memories for a family is another; writing is yet another still. There is a generosity of imagination in Gunn's depiction of what shape familial fruitfulness takes: from giving birth to giving forth. Some people grow people, some grow gardens, some grow language. 'Help me, Lord, to be satisfied.'

If this is a poem about hunger, pleasure, skill, business acumen and survival, it is also a poem about poetry. Amanda Gunn may not make the graham cracker cake, or fudge, but she has the notes, the writing of them. The invocation of the food's taste – I notice that I salivate when I read about the fudge, the sweet potato pie, the starches turned to caramel – is the first preservation, the canning is the second, and the language is the third. The poet needed to learn patience from a mother who 'taught [her] gently' the art of baking, of slicing 'fat into cold flour', of unfurling crust, but she has also discerned how patience and time work in writing. This poem spans decades, and may have taken that long to write. It provides recipes for fine cakes and pies alongside ingredients for life: love, admiration, survival, skill, repetition, practice, provision, tending the earth, tending each other, remembering the dead, keeping their words, 'pressed in a book / and safe.'

Family is a powerful word, one that evokes warmth for many. Families come in all forms, and all these shapes summon memories of sharing: whether of rooms, houses, resources, meals, bedrooms, bathrooms, opinions, decisions or time. In such proximity, all kinds of things are said to each other. Shared households can be a hotbed for intensified communication. When explosions happen – as explosions do – the language used is replete with information: about the target, but also about the one doing the targeting. To pay attention to the language you use with those around whom you don't watch your language is a revealing thing.

The Coup
Valencia Robin

My mother in all her armor
which so rarely came off – her laws, her decrees,
her look that said, *Don't ask me for anything*
before I could ask for anything, that roared
Off with her head! when I asked anyway.
Thus once – in a rare show of defiance – I said,
Then I want to call my father.
And even now I can't believe the words came out of my mouth.
My father, a man my mother had never acknowledged,
whose absence was treated no differently in our house
than, say, not having a cat or washer and dryer.
She looked terrified, like a dictator threatened with a coup,
like a lonely despot betrayed by her most trusted servant,
like a single mother, catching three buses to work,
no idea how she could be the bad guy.

In fifteen lines Valencia Robin's 'The Coup' portrays a scene of tension between a teenager and her mother. I say teenager because I'm assuming the speaker was one: someone, at least, who was old enough to desire fierce independence, but unable to leave. The mother's a force in the household: 'her laws, her decrees, / her look that said, *Don't ask me for anything* / before I could ask for anything, that roared . . .'

What's depicted is a recognisable relationship, one of tension, dedication, vulnerability, control and shock. The defiance, when it comes, is 'a rare show': the poet may have learnt not to voice it often. It may be that she didn't often dare. Or that she simply didn't know she had it in her. 'And even now I can't believe the words came out of my mouth.'

Combat is everywhere: 'all her armor / which so rarely came off', and those 'decrees'. The mother is like a 'dictator' or a 'lonely despot' or like *Alice in Wonderland*'s Queen of Hearts roaring '*Off with her head!*' What kind of a relationship is this? Tense, yes, but not violent. Loving, also, but also not easy. Valencia Robin dedicates the book in which the poem appears – *Ridiculous Light* – to her mother. 'The Coup', then, is a stage of this fundamental relationship; a true stage, necessary perhaps, not final.

The speaker's shock at her own words matches the mother's shock when she hears them. Valencia Robin summons the absent: '*Then I want to call my father.*' Why? What was the argument that led to this? What was the fantasised recourse that would have been appealed to? What on earth would he have said? The dream is that he'd declare *I'm on your side*; the nightmare is that he'd ask *Who's this?* If the mother–daughter relationship was, at that time, a battle, then the daughter's words seems less like a strategy and more like a dig. How did she know to say what she said? How did she summon the strange courage to say it? '*My father . . .* / whose absence was treated no differently in our house / than, say, not having a cat or washer and dryer.' I keep on seeing the 'our' before 'house'. This mother – this dictator, despot, provider in the face of absence – is so present as to be taken for granted. There was no cat, no washer and dryer, but there were walls, a kitchen, rules, three jobs, buses, a belief that despite the strictness, she wasn't 'the bad guy.' She is everywhere, surrounding the life of her daughter with opportunity, guidance, opinion and attention, when it was desired and when it was not.

The teenage part of me recalls the outrage at feeling contained. Nearing fifty now, with plenty of my friends whose children are that age, I see the wrath of independent desire in those young people. I believe it all: I'm sure their parents are inadequate just as I'm sure the offspring are offputting, I'm sure they'd die for each other, I'm sure they do everything they can. Welcome to the battle and to belonging.

There's a word I hate, even though I find it helpful sometimes. *Liminality.* I hate it because I heard it used so often during a particular time of my life that I have loaded my own hostility onto its five syllables. In fact, I even have an essay in a book on the damned concept. 'I'm compiling a book of essays on liminality,' a man said to me once, 'and you're Irish, and that's a deep concept in your culture. Could you write an essay?' If there's one thing I dislike more than liminality, it's the misty-eyed assumption that Irish people, like mystical leprechauns, have a relationship to the concept. 'I hate that word,' I said to him. Uncowed – what an opportunist! – he said 'well that's the perfect reason to write the essay!' I admitted defeat, and gave him my respect. He knew what he wanted, and won the battle.

The word itself means 'threshold' – the space between two rooms. It's a practical and physical word. If you stand under the doorframe of a house, you're in the *liminis*, the place between two places, part of you present to each. Valencia Robin's teenage self – this poem feels so autobiographical I hesitate to say 'the speaker' – is in a liminal location: her mother is provider and dictator; she herself is demure and defiant. The mother is liminal too: living a life oriented toward survival, her long days centred around providing the structures of love, 'no idea how she could be the bad guy.' There's no resolution given at the end: we're left on the cliff edge of self-questioning. That's part of the art.

I admire the similes throughout 'The Coup'. A simile categorises things alongside each other, saying something's *like, but not equivalent* to something else. To make a simile – 'like a dictator threatened with a coup' – is to engage in the complicated art of category. A simile is a vehicle, designed to take you somewhere, and although no simile is perfect, a good one contains vital information. I think Robin's use of adjective is magnificent in the line 'like a lonely despot betrayed by her most trusted servant': two points of view are possible. I can almost hear the daughter's voice saying 'you're a despot who treats me like a servant' at the same time that I can hear the response: 'I'm lonely and I trust you.'

The tension and truth of these parallel points of view electrify the tension between the characters.

Three similes support this short punch of a poem, and the final is the most powerful: 'like a single mother'. I hear the wisdom of time between the teenaged and adult writer as 'The Coup' ends. Now, rather than military comparisons, another category is used: the mother is like a mother, is like herself: a responsible, providing adult who is loving and trying.

A friend of mine was walking in a Melbourne park. She saw a woman sitting alone on a bench and – she wasn't sure why – went immediately and purchased flowers for the stranger.

My friend presented the flowers to the woman on the bench, somewhat apologetically. *Nobody knows it's my birthday*, the woman said, and *how did you know pansies are my favourite?*

Of course my friend didn't know. Of course she had no certitude. Of course.

Also, of course she felt something, and of course her response was filled with the generosity for which her friends love her.

All of this happened. I do not know how.

Three Mangoes, £1

Kandace Siobhan Walker

You know the dead are never dead / because I saw my
mum's mum / walking down Lewisham High Street / she
was wearing purple / she's always wearing purple / tak-
ing bites out of unripe mangoes / replacing them with the
other fruit / either she was invisible to the market ven-
dors / or unimaginable / the same thing really / our dead
couldn't stay dead even if they wanted to / what we call a
legacy / her voice / when she spoke / sounded tinny with
a hair-raising intimacy // we met last in a Toronto suburb
/ I remember / nothing about her / except pearls, deep
violet dress / full wig of violent / shine curls / her home
smelled like clean magic / fans running in every room /
but she wouldn't open the windows / afraid we'd let the
dead back / in / as if they hadn't made it through cus-
toms in our suitcases / her figure wavered / a telephone
line with a fault / her death too was technical / speaking
nothing of the bloated cancers / marbled purple calves /
decaying waterlogged feet / an email / with her name in
the subject line // just the Barbadian man from Waltham-
stow recognised iron in the air / her smell / like an an-
imal wound / he looked up, put a mango in a wrinkled
blue bag / his smile was not without empathy // for free
/ he said / there's no way to bury these things / earth will
only spit it back out / he must've known / he said eat /
in the park / it's a day / neither fine nor good / just a day

A Freudian slip happens when you mean one thing but say your mother. Perhaps a child calls their teacher *Dad* or an innuendo pops out when you mean to be decorous. But a Freudian slip can also be visual: you're walking down the road and you see someone who looks *just like* that person who died a year ago, a month ago. *Slip* in this context isn't referring to a mistake, the slip is that you slipped into the truth: of your desire, your yearning, your ache. So you call for your dad at a time when you most want him; you say something sexual at a time when sex isn't meant to be on your mind but is; or you feel the ghost of a grandmother while food shopping in a city street.

Kandace Siobhan Walker's 'Three Mangoes, £1' begins in the southeast of London, where she sees her 'mum's mum / walking down Lewisham High Street'. From the opening line, we know that two things are happening: she saw what she shouldn't – or couldn't – see: 'You know the dead are never dead / because I saw my mum's mum'. A ghost then, a here and a not-here. Alive and dead. Seen and unseen. Did she see someone who resembled her grandmother? Or did she just see where she would have been had she still been alive? Maybe it was in a stranger's gait, or deportment, or the angle at which she tilted her head. However the absent grandmother was called, she arrived: 'wearing purple / taking bites out of unripe mangoes'.

We turn to the dead often, especially in the early days of

grief. A friend of mine was very close to her father, and on the day he died – suddenly, shockingly – she found herself picking up the phone to text him to tell him the awful news. There is love and truth in this seeming mistake: she wished to be the one to tell him he'd died. The afterlife of questions appears in ways at once taunting and tangible. Who else would understand the depth of her sadness? She wanted his comfort too. He was a lovely man, he'd have dropped everything to show care.

Do the dead know they're dead, even though they're 'never dead'? These are questions that concern the living, we who still turn to them, still see them, still smell and feel their presences. And here's Kandace Siobhan Walker on a street, seeing what she cannot see. The grandmother 'invisible' or 'unimaginable' to all except her.

The poem moves: from London to a Toronto suburb, from fruit stalls in a city street to a home that 'smelled like clean magic / fans running in every room'. The 'Barbadian man from Walthamstow', too, calls locale to mind: one place conjures up another and a person carries ghosts with them. Places are portals: the grandmother 'wouldn't open the windows / afraid we'd let the dead back / in /'. Borders are called 'customs', not an unusual term for international frontiers in British English, but also evocative of other customs – of habit, of practice, of dress; fear of the dead too, even though the dead come calling.

Telephones bridge distant places with the evocative magic of a voice. On the phone, a person seems near and far at the same time: 'her voice / when she spoke / sounded tinny with a hair-raising intimacy'. *Tin* and *intimate*; the sound of the first word jumbled – almost inside out – in the first syllable of the second, and then repeated, just a shade off: tin, int, tim . . . *was that my grandmother going down the street just now, wearing purple?* Sounds and sights allude to one another, colluding in a sense of presence and echo. Echoes are voiced in alliteration too: 'my mum's mum', 'our dead couldn't stay dead'. And then there's that extraordinarily subtle echo of 'death' in 'technical'.

The block-shape of 'Three Mangoes, £1' is punctuated with / slashes //, some single, some double. These occur sometimes at the end of the line, sometimes midline. They create a certain breathlessness (like death) for anyone reading the poem, while also accelerating in tempo. The scenes change dramatically in the cinematic, dreamscape second-half: from a suitcase to a wavering figure, a faulty phone, a description of a death – 'the bloated cancers / marbled purple calves / decaying waterlogged feet' – then back to a medium of communication again: 'an email / with her name in the subject line'. The grandmother is the subject of a piece of flat communication, but is also walking after death, alive and playful, in the peripheral vision of the granddaughter. 'You know the dead are never dead': who is saying this? Kandace, or the purple-wearing, unripe-mango-biting mother's mother?

I love the Barbadian guy. What a man of attunement. He recognises the scent of iron. In Walker's art, she sketches him with generosity and care: he sees, he smells blood and wounds in the air, and he discerns grief. '[H]e must've known' – of course he did. And in response, he places an offering in a bag – 'his smile was not without empathy' – then says: 'for free'. We never hear what griefs and visitations he's known. In contrast to the grandmother, his presence is concrete, direct, and his communication unambiguous and clear. From his hand, the titular mango is reintroduced – unripe no longer, edible now – and he places it the hand of the bereaved. He is a voice of sense, not just because he gives her something tangible to do – 'he said eat' – but because he is present. Language had begun unravelling in the sometimes bewildering catalogue of cancer's symptoms. In the Barbadian man's company, language restitches itself into comprehensibility and tangibility: sight, smell, touch, smile, speech, and a reassurance that a granddaughter had been seen. He brings her back into the realm of the living, charming her back from the borderlands of the dead: on 'a day / neither fine nor good / just a day'.

Where do you carry shame in your body? There are some people who don't, and I praise the planet they live upon, but it is not a planet I have inhabited. For me – and for so many, I know – shame is a story told to ourselves. It inhibits the space between us, the space we live in for ourselves. Shame can cause more shame: to cover it over can mean it's projected onto others. The story of my body's relationship to my own body – and the bodies of others – is a poem that's asking for my attention.

The change room
Andy Jackson

This morning, walking almost naked
from the change room toward the outdoor heated pool,
I become *that man* again, unsettling

shape to be explained.
Such questions aren't asked to my face. Children
don't mean anything by it, supposedly, so I

shouldn't feel as I do,
as my bones crouch into an old shame I thought
I'd left behind. Chlorine prickling

my nostrils, a stranger
compliments me on my tattoos and shows me hers –
a dove in flight over a green peace sign –

as if the canvas was unremarkable.
She turns and limps away,
and something makes a moment of sense.

I lower myself into our element
and swim, naturally
asymmetrical and buoyant. Quite some time

later, showering, the man beside me
is keen to chat – how many laps we've each done,
how long I've lived in this town, the deep

need for movement.
Speaking, our bodies become solid.

'The change room' of Andy Jackson's title opens a door into a room of many possibilities. There is the changing room at a swimming pool, yes. But the poem also looks at how many rooms change, depending as to who enters, or doesn't. Andy Jackson has a genetic condition called Marfan syndrome, which for him includes severe spinal curvature. He is aware that people's responses to his body – a body 'shaped like a question mark', as a tagline on his website states – change the dynamics of rooms he enters. Can a poem be a room that enacts change? Can the stanzas – the rooms – of poetry facilitate, or provoke, change in the lives of its readers? That's one of the questions we're left with as 'The change room' unfolds.

The simple narrative structure – a man walks from the changing room to the pool, is subjected to the classifying gaze of one person, has a conversation about tattoos with another, leaves the pool and showers beside a chatty man – is not the sum total of the work. Rather the scenes point to how body language is part of every human experience, an experience that's made particularly pointed for those whose bodies are subjected to comment.

In 'The change room' we read of nostrils, skin, tattoos, gaits, swimming, floating, showering, nakedness, proximity, speaking: all parts, functions and experiences of the body, all vehicles for body language, all ways in which the body is in conversation with itself and others. The speaker enters the poem 'walking', 'almost naked' and 'become[s]' something else: an 'unsettling // shape to be explained'. To be explained to whom? Someone who considers their body to meet a set of criteria his doesn't, even if that person is a child. We know that the body is not just the body, it is also a container for emotion and experience, and to be judged for your body is to be judged for your being: 'bones crouch into an old shame'. Shame is a burden heaped upon a person, and yet it is learnt so young.

'The change room' is part of the award-winning 2021 collection *Human Looking* – a title rich with multiple interpretations: *looking* as verb, as in 'a human is looking'; or *looking* as a modifier, as in looking *somewhat like but not entirely* human. If his body is shaped like a question mark, then what's the answer to that question? A plea – *please accept me, please accept me, please accept me* – is not a question; it's an indication of exclusion. The question, perhaps, is 'Who is anyone to decide if anyone else is human-looking enough?'. 'The change room' is not just about what's narrated in the body of the poem, rather it's about the world in which the action occurs; a world that repeats itself and repeats itself in room after room. The 'change' of the title may be an imperative: an order, a demand, an invitation to those who need to change to step into a room where true change may happen.

When referring to the questions that arise – but are unvoiced – in his presence, I admire the truth revealed in the line 'Children / don't mean anything by it, supposedly'. This is someone who bears the burden of questions – spoken or not – and, I'm guessing, has heard that he must bear the burden of pardoning those who lay the weight of their projection upon him. *Supposedly* pushes back, and says that perhaps people, whatever their age, *do* mean something by their questions: is he human or only human-*looking*? Anyway, even with such critique the language shows us where the weight lands: that 'old shame I thought / I'd left behind.' How interesting that shame is associated with crouching, making oneself smaller, perhaps wishing to be less notice-able, or hidden away. Here he is, 'almost naked', outdoors: confident enough to choose to be there, aware enough to anticipate the unaired projections on himself, aware enough, too, to stand as a query point to the presumption behind such projections.

There follow what I think of as three turns. The first turn is signalled by the arrival of a stranger who compliments the poet's tattoos. Her attention has been caught by some-thing else – the shapes inked upon his body, not the shape of his body. When she 'limps away . . . something makes a moment of sense', and perhaps he understands why she understands. The second turn is private and intimate and solitary: he gets into the water – 'our element' he calls it, conjuring the primordial soup out of which all living beings came, calling to mind the amniotic fluid in which we all were suspended – and his swimming is 'naturally / asymmetrical and buoyant.' There's a linebreak after 'naturally' which leaves us with the straight line: 'and swim, naturally'. *Naturally*: an adverb meaning *according to nature*. This frag-ment, midway through a sentence, is an assertion of truth that he knows, and that the water supports.

Later, the third turn: he showers beside a chatty man who wants to know about him, his laps, his longevity in the town. Body next to body. Different. Other. In conversation. Their topics are everyday, but the exchange is held up by the psychological insight of 'the deep // need for movement':

movement in water, movement in growing up, movement in being able to relate, movement in going from depth to depth.

'Speaking, our bodies become solid', the poem ends. 'Bodies' here are held in a plural pronoun 'our'. Why have they become solid? Were they not before? Were they fluid, or see-through, or gaseous? Perhaps solid is meant as the antonym for unreliable. The final stanza is composed only of two lines, in comparison with the seven tercets that preceded it. The missing third line of the last invites, perhaps, buoyancy, nature, exchange, consideration among all the bodies in, and reading a poem about, 'The change room'. The poem asserts a shameless body-knowledge it establishes for itself.

I've sometimes found my thinking to be clearest when I'm grieving: someone's died; something's over; something's gone. Grief is accompanied by its own emptiness, yes; but it also opens doors.

Once, after grief, I found myself able to donate books I thought I'd never let go of. Another time, in another bereavement, I was able to say something I thought I'd never be able to say.

There are many poems about many types of grief. Such works not only describe what is lost, they also describe what can – finally – be seen. Nobody would choose grief as a pathway to insight, but we don't get the choice; the wisdom gained can be invaluable.

Fear and Love

Jim Moore

I wish I could make the argument that a river
and a sunset plus a calm disregard of the ego
are enough. But whatever comes next must include
tents in the parking lot, that homeless camp
on the way to the airport,
and the hole in your cheek
from the cancer removed yesterday.
I said last night,
in the few seconds before I fell asleep,
You do realize, don't you, everything
is falling apart? You said, *OK,*
I'll try to keep that in mind. And now it is
starting to be late again, just like every other night
for the last seventy-five years. *Fear and love,*
a friend said in an impromptu speech
at his surprise birthday party,
we all live caught between fear and love.
He tried to smile as he spoke, then sat down.
Yesterday you saw the moon
from the operating table
where they were about to cut you.
Look! you demanded, and the surgeon bent and turned
to see it from your angle,
knife in hand.

Visiting my friend Marie once, she took a book from her shelf, handed it to me, and said 'give it back once you've read it.' It was a collection of Jim Moore's poetry. I read it. Twice. Then bought a copy of it before giving it back. His poems work on the level of revelation: showing truth through concrete scenes that point beyond themselves. In sequence, everyday language, and lines unadorned by artifice, he speaks with wisdom and trust.

I've tried, a few times, to remove *trust* from the previous sentence, but I can't. Moore's poetry trusts the reader in a way that elicits some shared level of humanity, concern and care. He speaks as an individual, a man in later life, a citizen, a friend, a partner, someone with yearning, shortcomings, and love. There's a moral imagination in his work demonstrated especially here. The language that emerges from such integrity draws the reader in. 'Fear and Love' functions not only as a title, but also a spectrum and summary. The speaker – at least 'seventy-five years' of age – is considering 'whatever comes next'. Death has granted focus to his attention. He cannot be satisfied with what has given merely personal guidance and satisfaction: 'a river / and a sunset plus a calm disregard of the ego' are inadequate. Inner ease is no longer enough, and the speaker wishes to take in as much reality as he can: those who are failed by circumstances, and those who are facing what seems unsolvable: 'that homeless camp / on the way to the airport.'

Is this hopelessness in the face of life's end? A sense of feeling powerless before the inevitable? There is only one answer to this: yes. In the twenty-four lines of 'Fear and Love' is the plain reality that death awaits us all. It's directly narrated in the depiction of 'the hole in your cheek / from the cancer removed yesterday'. But it occurs obliquely in other metaphors: 'in the few seconds before I fell asleep'; *everything / is falling apart*; 'sunset'; the oncoming night 'late again', and especially that final image, the shortest line in the entire poem: 'knife in hand'. Different people live with death differently: some rarely think about it; others are visited by it every day, and not in ways that are necessarily morose. 'Death and taxes' are the consistencies of life, I heard, but Jim Moore believes differently. In the face of death, and the cruel disparities of housing irregularity, he proposes 'Fear and Love' as a summation of what's important; not because they eradicate death, but because they are the necessary conditions and concerns for the living.

Reading the poem, I feel like I was in attendance at that party where the impromptu speech took place: 'He tried to smile as he spoke, then sat down.' I can see it. I can feel it, too: the bravery of language, the kindness of the smile. A friend was in a hospital bed a few years ago and said 'I couldn't give that lecture this year, but I'll give it next year.' Everybody – including him – knew he'd die far sooner. He looked around, his skinny legs curled up underneath the hospital blanket. He smiled, just like the man at the party. Not out of defiance, perhaps just because he could, or maybe it was a gesture of generosity to those of us around his bed. To bear witness to a friend's body and language when they're carrying the weight of time is a form of love that moves me deeply. The poem's party was a surprise, perhaps age and realisation are too. '*[W]e all live caught between fear and love*' the friend said. And his friends heard his words, perceived the many meanings in what he communicated, and presumably were glad for the chair to bear the body that was finding it hard to bear itself and everything it contained.

There are many contrasts in 'Fear and Love', a short work included in Moore's most recent publication *Prognosis* – a telling title. The speaker does not share personal medical health, whereas the beloved has cancer. He's the one saying '*everything / is falling apart*' but his companion seems more interested in alleviating those catastrophising tendencies. '*OK, / I'll try to keep that in mind*' comes across with easy affection: words spoken by someone who understands their partner's tendency to worry, even wishes to calm it, yet not share it. Fear weighing on one, love on the other. Love between them too: for the world, themselves, time and shared life. The contrasts – whether of health or ill-health, parties or surgeries, fear or love – do not invite the reader to judge. The poem demonstrates how worry and ease are located in tangible experiences or objects: the river, the sunset, tents, camps, airports, cheeks with cancer, the moon, the operating table, the knife, the hand that holds the knife.

'Fear and Love' depicts the crisis of inevitability in a series of elegant transitions. 'I wish I could' the speaker begins, and we are introduced to a pragmatist who is no longer satisfied with personal calm, but one who wants to inhale the world. Then the direction of the lines moves from description to address – 'your cheek' – before bringing us into the intimate domesticity of a couple's bedtime conversation. There follows that party and the impromptu speech of a friend. Then back to what was foreshadowed: the cutting room, the night 'the moon / from the operating table', the surgeon-stranger performing an act of salvation, a sharp instrument into the soft skin of a face where one might place a kiss. The transitions flow with the simplicity of conversation and the characters' points of view are contrasted elegantly: the speaker takes in the impoverishment of inadequate housing provision; the beloved – the 'you' – is not unaware of death, but has a different relationship to time, finding the moon even in the surgery, capable of compelling the surgeon to obey the demand of '*Look!*'

When I was growing up, there was a priest in our parish, a sometimes grumpy man. Mostly I avoided him.

Once, in my late teens, I was early for a weekday Mass and he came over and sat next to me. He seemed exhausted. He began talking, saying he'd been in a death house the night before, a home that had been visited by a sudden grief. 'People say the priest's job is words,' he said, 'but it's not, it's silence. I sat at the table all night, in case they needed me. I'm here now for Mass and then I might get a bit of sleep.'

Hebrews 13
Jericho Brown

Once, long ago, in a land I cannot name,
My lover and my brother both knocked
At my door like wind in an early winter.
I turned the heat high and poured coffee
Blacker than their hands which shivered
As we sat in silence so thin I had to hum.
They drank with a speed that must have
Burned their tongues one hot cup then
Another like two bitter friends who only
Wished to be warm again like two worn
Copies of a holy book bound by words to keep
Watch over my life in the cold and never ever sleep

What a twelve-line punch is 'Hebrews 13'. Examining its shape on the page, we see ten justified lines of almost equal length followed by two final lines – 'keep' and 'sleep' rhyming.

Jericho Brown is a poet of extraordinary lyricism, whose musical lines communicate in sonic and emotional registers. Often elegiac, his poetry combines longing and lament to build a disarming affect. 'Hebrews 13' achieves this, right from the mythical – yet slightly reframed – beginning: 'Once, long ago'. A fairytale start perhaps, but not *in a land far, far away*, rather 'in a land I cannot name'.

What is unnameable? Shame, as a feature of human experience, turns the volume up on something you'd rather not hear, while simultaneously turning the volume down on sharing. To be in a state of shame is to pay attention to a story you wish to reject, while attempting to reject the story you're paying attention to. Shame is an experience of conflict: to be under it is to find yourself giving profound attention to something you don't want to believe. There are numerous counterspells to shame: telling the truth being one of them, presence being another. 'Hebrews 13' uses such magic to dignify that which language demeaned.

The second line opens with two characters – 'My lover and my brother' – bonded in love for the speaker, as well as in a certain rhyme. They 'both knocked / At my door like wind' and the fairytale continues: knocks, door, inclement weather outside like a portent of doom. They're shivering, and they need the 'coffee / Blacker than their hands'. Why are they shivering? From the weather? From anxiety? From not knowing what to do even though they are there? They take strength from one burning cup and then another.

The majusculation of these lines – the capital letter down the left-hand column of the poem's body – adds an air of formality to the shape. And the title is a reference to the final chapter of the Letter to the Hebrews, an epistle of unknown authorship contained in the Christian New Testament. The thirteenth chapter commences with the following words: 'Let mutual love continue. Do not neglect to show hospitality to strangers, for by doing that some have entertained angels without knowing it. Remember those who are in prison, as though you were in prison with them; those who are being tortured, as though you yourselves were being tortured.' It is a chapter of immense psychological insight, offering patterns and behaviours of love as a way of demonstrating faith. Jericho Brown is a gay Black man whose poetry evidences his interests in religious language and 'Hebrews 13' is published in his collection titled *The New Testament*. The new testament of what? Shapes and experiences of love demonstrated between people whose allegiance to other interpretations of their testament would otherwise have separated them?

Almost half of this short poem is taken up with simile: it is used to describe the sound of the visitors' knocks, the colour of their skin, the awkwardness of this gathering, the need for warmth, the shared love for the narrator. The desire to try – again and again – to find the vehicle that can adequately explain their attendance demonstrates how even words aren't good enough to describe their silent, loving vigil.

But why, amidst the many similes and adjacencies that could have been used, are the brother and lover 'like two bitter friends'? Has their concern joined them together in a way that would otherwise have seemed unlikely? Love seems like a soft skill in the realm of relational resolution, but it is one of the primal driving forces in us. Love does have the capacity to help those who would ordinarily have been divided to sit, side by side in the heat provided by someone they both love, even though they do not love each other. Not yet anyway. The simile of bitter friends evolves into that of 'two worn / Copies of a holy book'. Their script becomes similar – that of love for the man behind the door.

There is no 'happily ever after' here, but there is something more: loving silent vigilance – the two visitors 'never ever sleep' despite the cold. No wonder they needed the 'heat high' and 'one hot cup then / Another'. Perhaps they had no words for each other, but found that their bodies could communicate a mutual endeavour where their differences would merely have separated. Language is communicated by body: their presence is their language.

It can be a difficult thing to realise I need help. And then, even when I realise I need help, I can avoid asking for it because of shame. The speaker in 'Hebrews 13', too, is in need. This could seem like a state of weakness, and – in one reading of the economics of the self – it may be. However, something else is happening too: someone is in need, and his need is great enough to make unlikely men reconcile. Power is revealed in unexpected ways. The narrator of the poem is the gathering point for divided men. The archetypes of brother and lover could be understood as welcoming the familial as well as the erotic through your door, inviting them to sit, and bearing witness to a life that can contain both devotion and desire.

Notes on the Poets

Mosab Abu Toha is a Palestinian poet, columnist, and academic whose work has appeared in *The Nation,* the *New York Times* and the *New Yorker*. Born in Gaza, he is the founder of the Edward Said Library, an English-language public library in Beit Laha. He has an MFA in poetry from the University of Syracuse, and from 2019–2020 he was a Scholar-at-Risk Fellow in the Department of Comparative Literature at Harvard Divinity School. His collection *Things You May Find Hidden in My Ear: Poems from Gaza* was published by City Lights in 2022. He fled Gaza with his family in November 2023. HIs collection *Forest of Noise* was released by Knopf in 2024.

Nico Amador is a poet, essayist, educator and community organiser from San Diego in the USA. He was named Peace Educator of the Year by the Peace and Justice Studies Association in 2017. His chapbook, *Flower Wars*, won the Anzaldúa Poetry Prize and was published by Newfound Press in 2017. He lives in rural Vermont, in the United States.

Caroline Bird is an English poet and playwright whose works include *The Trojan Women* and *The Trial of Dennis the Menace*. She has written six collections of poetry, the first when she was fifteen. Her collection, *The Air Year*

(Carcanet, 2020), won multiple accolades: it was named Book of the Year by the *Telegraph* and the *Guardian*, and awarded a Forward Prize. She was president of the Oxford Poetry Society, and an official poet at the London 2012 Olympics. Her collection *Ambush at Still Lake* was released in 2024.

Richard Blanco is a poet, performer, and engineer, who was born in Madrid to parents exiled from Cuba, and raised in Miami, in the USA. His numerous accolades include a National Humanities Medal, a Maine Literary Award, and an Agnes Lynch Starrett Poetry Prize; he was also appointed as the first Education Ambassador of the Academy of American Poets. He performed at the inauguration of President Barrack Obama in 2013, the first immigrant and Latino to do so. His collection *Homeland of My Body: New & Selected Poems* was released by Beacon Press in October 2023.

Jericho Brown is an American writer whose work has appeared in *Time* magazine, the *Paris Review*, and the *New Yorker*. He has been awarded fellowships by the Guggenheim Foundation, the National Endowment for the Arts, and the Radcliffe Institute for Advanced Study at Harvard University. His third poetry collection, *The Tradition* (Copper Canyon Press, 2019), won a Pulitzer Prize and was a finalist for the National Book Award. He is a professor and the director of the Creative Writing Program at Emory University in Georgia.

Colette Bryce is a poet from Derry in the north of Ireland. She was a Fellow in Creative Writing at the University of Dundee from 2003–2005, and the poetry editor of *Poetry London* from 2009–2013. She is the recipient of an Eric Gregory Award, a Cholmondeley Award, and a Ewart-Biggs

Memorial Prize. *The Whole & Rain-domed Universe* was published by Picador in 2014.

M. Soledad Caballero is a Chilean-American poet, essayist, and academic, whose work has featured in publications including the *Missouri Review* and the *Iron Horse Literary Review*. She is a professor of English and chair of the Women's Gender and Sexuality Studies programme at Allegheny College in Pennsylvania. Her collection *I Was a Bell* (Red Hen Press, 2021) was awarded a Juan Felipe Herrera Award by the International Latino Book Awards.

C.P. Cavafy (Greek: Konstantinos Petrou Kavafis) was a Greek poet and journalist who was born in Alexandria in 1863. During his lifetime, his work appeared primarily in local newspapers and privately published collections, or was circulated among friends. His work has been translated into many languages: more than twenty English translation collections of his work have been published since his death in 1933.

Chen Chen is a writer and editor. He completed an MFA at Syracuse University in the United States and a PhD in English and Creative Writing at Texas Tech University. Among other accolades, he is the recipient of a National Endowment for the Arts Fellowship, two Pushcart Prizes, and a Thom Gunn Award for Gay Poetry. His second collection of poetry, *Your Emergency Contact Has Experienced an Emergency*, was published by BOA Editions and Bloodaxe Books in 2022.

John Lee Clark is an American DeafBlind poet, essayist, translator, activist, and educator. In 2020, he was the recipient of a Disability Futures Fellowship, awarded by the Ford and Mellon Foundations, and for his 2019 essay 'Tactile Art' (*Poetry*), he won a National Magazine Award. His collection *How to Communicate* (W. W. Norton, 2022) won a Minnesota Book Award.

Tiana Clark is an American poet, essayist and academic. Her work has appeared in the *Washington Post*, the *Atlantic*, *American Poetry Review* and the *New Yorker*, and been featured in the Academy of American Poets' Poem-a-Day. She has been awarded a Fellowship by the National Endowment for the Arts and a Pushcart Prize. Her second collection of poetry, *I Can't Talk About the Trees Without the Blood*, won the Agnes Lynch Starrett Poetry Prize, and was published by the University of Pittsburgh Press in 2018.

Lucille Clifton (1936–2010) was an American poet and children's author. She published thirteen collections of poems and was a Pulitzer Prize finalist on two occasions. She held positions at the University of California, Dartmouth College and Columbia University, and was the Poet Laureate of Maryland from 1979–1985. She also served on the board of chancellors of the Academy of American Poets. In 2010, she was chosen as the Poetry Society of America's Centennial Frost Medallist. *The Collected Poems of Lucille Clifton* was published by BOA Editions in 2012.

The English poet **Wendy Cope** has published numerous collections of poetry, including *Making Cocoa for Kingsley Amis* (Faber and Faber, 1986), *Serious Concerns* (Faber and Faber, 1992) and *If I Don't Know* (Faber and Faber, 2001), which was nominated for the Whitbread Poetry Award. She has also written for publications including the *Telegraph* and the *Guardian*. She received a Michael Braude Award for Light Verse from the American Academy of Arts and Letters, and is a Fellow of the Royal Society of Literature in Britain.

Tishani Doshi is an Indian poet and novelist. She won the All-India Poetry Competition in 2005, and was awarded a Forward Prize for her debut poetry collection, *Countries of the Body* (HarperCollins India, 2006). She is Visiting Associate Professor of Practice, Literature and Creative Writing at New York University in Abu Dhabi, and a Fellow of the Royal Society of Literature. Her most recent collection, *A God at the Door*, was published by Bloodaxe Books in 2021.

Rita Dove is an American poet, essayist and fiction writer. She was the Poet Laureate of the United States from 1993–1995, and has written poetry columns for *New York Times Magazine* and the *Washington Post*. Her poetry collections include *On the Bus with Rosa Parks* (Norton, 1999) and *Thomas and Beulah* (Carnegie Mellon University Press, 1986), for which she was awarded a Pulitzer Prize in 1987. In 2021, she received a Gold Medal for Poetry from the American Academy of Arts and Letters; she has served as vice president for literature at the Academy since 2023.

Denise Duhamel is a distinguished professor in English at Florida International University in the USA. She has received fellowships from the Guggenheim Foundation and the National Endowment for the Arts. Her 2013 collection, *Blowout* (University of Pittsburgh Press), was a finalist for the National Book Critics Circle Award.

Safia Elhillo is a Sudanese-American poet. She is the recipient of a Ruth Lilly and Dorothy Sargent Rosenberg Fellowship and a Brunel International African Poetry Prize.

Her debut collection, *The January Children* (University of Nebraska Press, 2017), won an Arab American Book Award and the Sillerman First Book Prize for African Poets. Her work has been featured at TEDx New York, in *Poetry*, and in the Academy of American Poets' Poem-a-Day.

Nick Flynn is an American playwright, poet, and non-fiction writer whose work has appeared in the *New Yorker*, the *Paris Review*, and the Academy of American Poets' Poem-a-Day. He is the recipient of fellowships from the Guggenheim Foundation and the Library of Congress. His most recent collection, *Low*, was published by Graywolf Press in 2023.

Zuzanna Ginczanka was a Polish-Jewish poet born in Kyiv in 1917. Only one collection of her poetry, *O centaurach*, was published in her lifetime; in 1944 she was arrested in Kraków and killed by the Gestapo. An English-language translation of her work, *On Centaurs & Other Poems* (translated by Alex Braslavsky), was published by World Poetry Books in 2023.

The American poet **Benjamin Gucciardi** is the author of two chapbooks and the collection *West Portal* (University of Utah Press, 2021), which was awarded the Agha Shahid Ali Prize in Poetry. He is also the recipient of a Dorothy Sargent Rosenberg Prize. His work has appeared in *American Poetry Review* and *Harvard Review*.

Amanda Gunn is an American poet and editor. She is the recipient of a Wallace Stegner Fellowship at Stanford University, and was awarded a writing fellowship by the Civitella Ranieri Foundation. Her work has appeared in *Poetry*, the *Kenyon Review*, and *Los Angeles Review of*

Books. Her debut collection, *Things I Didn't Do with This Body*, was published by Copper Canyon Press in 2023.

Joy Harjo is a poet, musician and performer of the Muskogee (Creek) Nation. She has published several collections of poetry, as well as books of fiction for children and a memoir. She has been awarded the Ruth Lilly Poetry Prize for Lifetime Achievement by the Poetry Foundation and a Guggenheim Fellowship, among many other accolades. She was Poet Laureate of the United States from 2019–2022, becoming the first Native American poet to hold the position. She is a chancellor of the Academy of American Poets.

Robert Hayden (1913–1980) was an American poet and teacher who studied under W.H. Auden. He taught at Fisk University and the University of Michigan, and was visiting poet at institutions including the University of Washington. He published eight collections of poetry in his lifetime; a further two volumes of his collected works were published posthumously. He was the first African-American to be appointed as Consultant in Poetry to the Library of Congress (the title popularly known as Poet Laureate of the United States).

Langston Hughes (1901–1967) was an African-American poet, playwright, novelist, and columnist. In 1930, he was awarded a gold Harmon Foundation Award for his first novel, *Not Without Laughter* (Random House, 1930). His poetry has been widely translated, and has featured in other creative projects, including being set to music. For twenty years, he was a columnist for the *Chicago Defender*, and was inducted into the Chicago Literary Hall of Fame in 2012.

Joanna Trzeciak Huss is an academic, editor, and translator. For the collection *Miracle Fair: Selected Poems of Wisława Szymborska* (W. W. Norton, 2002) she was awarded a Heldt Prize. Her translations have appeared in publications including the *Atlantic*, *Virginia Quarterly Review*, and the *New York Times*. She is professor of Russian and Polish Translation at Kent State University, Ohio, United States.

Andy Jackson is an Australian poet preoccupied with difference, embodiment and solidarity. He has featured at literary events and arts festivals across Australia, in Ireland, India and the USA and works part-time as a lecturer in poetry and creative writing at the University of Melbourne. In 2022, his collection *Human Looking* won the Australian Prime Minister's Literary Award, and the Australian Literature Society Gold Medal.

Benjamín Naka-Hasebe Kingsley belongs to the Onondaga Nation of Indigenous Americans. He has published three collections of poetry; his work has also been featured in publications including *Rattle* and the *Kenyon Review*. He has been awarded fellowships by the Provincetown Fine Arts Work Center and Tickner Writing Center. His most recent collection, *Dēmos*, was published in 2021.

Sasha taqʷšəblu LaPointe is a writer of poetry and creative nonfiction from the Upper Skagit and Nooksack Indian Tribe. Her work has been featured in the *Rumpus* literary journal and the *Portland Review*. Her memoir, *Red Paint* (Counterpoint Press, 2022), won the 2023 Washington State Book Award and was named a Best Book of the Year by NPR.

Dorianne Laux's sixth collection, *Only As the Day Is Long: New and Selected Poems* was named a finalist for the 2020

Pulitzer Prize for Poetry. Her previous collections have won and been shortlisted for many prizes. She is the co-author of the celebrated text *The Poet's Companion: A Guide to the Pleasures of Writing Poetry*. She lives in North Carolina in the United States and in 2024, her latest collection *Life on Earth* was released.

Eugenia Leigh is a Korean-American poet whose work has appeared in numerous publications including the *Atlantic* and *Poetry Northwest*. She has published two collections of poetry; her first, *Blood, Sparrows, and Sparrows* (Four Way Books, 2014), won the Late Night Library's Debut-litzer Prize for Poetry in 2015. She has served as a teaching artist at numerous organisations, including the Asian American Legal Defense and Education Fund's group for undocumented youths.

Thomas Lux (1946–2017) was an American poet and academic. He was the founding director of Poetry@Tech and the inaugural Bourne Chair in Poetry at Georgia Institute of Technology. His collection *Split Horizon* (Houghton Mifflin, 1994) was awarded the Kingsley Tufts Poetry Award; he was also the recipient of a Guggenheim Fellowship and three grants from the National Endowment for the Arts, among many other accolades. He taught at institutions including the Universities of Iowa, Michigan and California, and was poet-in-residence at Emerson College from 1972–1975.

Philip Metres is an Arab-American writer of poetry, essays, fiction, and criticism. His work has been featured in the *Kenyon Review*, the *Margins* and *World Literature Today*, and he is the recipient of fellowships from the Guggenheim Foundation, the National Endowment for the Arts, and the

Ohio Arts Council. He is professor in the Department of English and director of the Peace, Justice, and Human Rights Program at John Carroll University in Ohio in the USA.

The American poet **Jim Moore** has published eight collections of poetry, and had work featured in publications including the *New Yorker* and the *Paris Review*. He is the recipient of a Guggenheim Fellowship, and a four-time winner of the Minnesota Book Award. He teaches at Hamline University in Minnesota and Colorado College in Colorado Springs. His most recent collection, *Prognosis*, was published by Graywolf Press in 2021.

In 1984, the American poet **Mary Oliver** (1935–2019) won a Pulitzer Prize for her collection *American Primitive*. Throughout her life she published over twenty volumes of poetry, many of which demonstrated her interest in animals, emotion, solitude, early mornings and the natural world. In addition to the Pulitzer, she won many awards, including the National Book Award, a Lannan Literary Award and a Guggenheim Foundation Fellowship. Born in Ohio, she spent much of her adult life in Provincetown, Massachusetts. Her partner Molly Malone Cook died in 2005, after which Mary Oliver published *Thirst*. In the following years, she moved to Florida, where she died in 2019.

Vidyan Ravinthiran was born in England to Sri Lankan Tamils. He is a poet, editor, and academic. His 2019 collection, *The Million-petalled Flower of Being Here* (Bloodaxe Books, 2019), won a Northern Writers Award and was a Poetry Book Society Recommendation. His work has been published in *Poetry*, the *Nation*, and the *Guardian*. He was awarded degrees by the Universities of Oxford and Cambridge, and is a professor in the Department of English at Harvard University.

Victoria Redel writes poetry, essays, and fiction. She has received fellowships from the Guggenheim Foundation, the National Endowment for the Arts, and the Fine Arts Work Center, and has written for publications including the *New York Times*, the *Los Angeles Times* and LitHub. Her most recent collection of poetry, *Paradise*, was published by Four Way Books in 2022. She teaches at Sarah Lawrence College in New York, USA.

Valencia Robin is a poet and artist whose writing has appeared in the *Boston Review* and the *New York Times*. She was awarded a fellowship by the National Endowment for the Arts in 2021. Her debut poetry collection, *Ridiculous Light* (Persea Books, 2019), was named one of *Library Journal*'s best poetry books of 2019. She is visiting professor of English at East Tennessee State University in the United States.

Patricia Smith is an American poet, playwright, and spoken-word performer. She has published eight collections of poetry and has won the National Poetry Slam championship on four occasions. Her work has been featured in *Poetry*, the *Paris Review*, and the *Washington Post.* Her awards include fellowships from the Guggenheim Foundation and the National Endowment for the Arts, two Pushcart Prizes, and the Ruth Lilly Poetry Prize for Lifetime Achievement.

Wisława Szymborska (1923–2012) was a Polish poet and essayist whose work has been translated into English, Hungarian, Danish and Hebrew, among many other languages. Her work has also been featured in music and in film. She won a Nobel Prize for Literature in 1996; her other awards included a Goethe Prize and the Order of the White Eagle.

Kai Cheng Thom is a Canadian writer, performer, arts facilitator, and conflict resolution practitioner. She is the recipient of awards including a Dayne Ogilvie Prize for LGBTQ Emerging Writers, and a Stonewall Honor Book Award for non-fiction. Her debut poetry collection, *a place called No Homeland*, was published by Arsenal Pulp Press in 2017.

Mark Turcotte grew up on Turtle Mountain Chippewa Reservation in North Dakota in the US. He writes poetry and short fiction, and his work has appeared in the Academy of American Poets' Poem-a-Day, the *Kenyon Review* and *Rosebud*. He has been awarded two literary fellowships by the Wisconsin Arts Board, and an award from the Wordcraft Circle of Native Writers and Storytellers. He is Distinguished Writer in Residence at DePaul University in Chicago.

Molly Twomey is an Irish poet and performer whose work has been featured in *Poetry Ireland Review*, *New England Review* and *Banshee*. Her debut poetry collection, *Raised Among Vultures* (The Gallery Press, 2022), won the Southword Debut Collection Poetry Award, and was named a book of the year by the *Irish Times*.

Alissa Valles is an author and translator. She has been a recipient of the *Poetry* magazine's Ruth Lilly Poetry Fellowship and the Bess Hokin Prize. For *NYRB*, she has translated, among other titles, Zuzanna Ginczana's *Firebird*. She lives in the US, between Boston and the Bay Area.

Laura Villareal is an American poet and book critic. She completed an MFA at Rutgers University, and writes for the Letras Latinas Blog 2 at the University of Notre Dame's Institute for Latino Studies. Her debut collection, *Girl's Guide to Leaving* (University of Wisconsin Press, 2022), was awarded a Texas Institute of Letters John A. Robert Johnson Award for a First Book of Poetry and the Writers' League of Texas Book Award for Poetry.

Kandace Siobhan Walker is a writer and artist of Canadian, Jamaican, Gullah-Geechee and Welsh heritage. Her work has appeared in numerous anthologies, been published in the *Guardian* and the *Poetry Review*, and been featured on BBC Radio 4. She is the recipient of an Eric Gregory Award and the *White Review*'s Poet's Prize. She has published two collections of poetry: *Kaleido* (Bad Betty Press, 2022), and *Cowboy* (CHEERIO Publishing, 2023) and lives in the UK.

Michael Wasson is a Nimíipuu poet from the Nez Perce Reservation in Idaho, USA. He has published two collections of poetry, and his work has appeared in publications including the *New York Times*, *Boston Review*, and the Academy of American Poets' Poem-a-Day. He is the recipient of a Ruth Lilly and Dorothy Sargent Rosenberg Fellowship and an Adrienne Rich Award for Poetry.

Acknowledgements

My deep thanks go to the beloved Krista Tippett, founder and president of On Being, with whom so much has developed over these years of the *Poetry Unbound* work. Alongside that, to the producers – particularly Gautam Srikishan, Chris Heagle and Kayla Edwards – who are so much part of the work. My other On Being colleagues, too, who have provided support, ideas, considerations, queries and joy, thank you: Lucas Johnson, Tiffany Champion, Zack Rose, Julie Siple, Andrea Prevost, Laurén Drommerhausen, Gretchen Honnold, Ashley Her, Eddie Gonzalez, Colleen Scheck, Cameron Mussar, Lil Vo, Annisa Hale, Erin Colasacco, Amy Chatelaine, Carla Zanoni, Daryl Chen, and the others along the way.

Thanks to my irreplaceable and wonderful and kind agent Clare Conville and everyone at C&W Agency, including Lizzie Milne and Darren Biabowe Barnes. Anya Backlund and all at Blue Flower deserve all praise, all the time. My deep love and thanks to Jamie Byng whose support of writing and writers is a thing of commitment and joy. Thanks to Silvie for the initial idea! And – as always – Patience Agbabi. Thank you to everyone at Canongate, especially Mel Tombere, Vicki Rutherford, Jamie Norman, Lucy Zhou and Jenny Fry. The folks at Riot are a riot, thank you. My deep love and gratitude to Jill Bialosky at W. W. Norton, whose editing skills and kindness run as deep as each other. Thank you, too, to all the others at Norton. Martha Sprackland should have a verb named after her for Spracklanding the manuscript as only she can, with precision and insight and wit and spark.

Support for the early development of this work came from the Morton Deutsch International Center for Cooperation and Conflict Resolution, as well as the Columbia Climate School, Abby Disney and other private donors. Peter Coleman and Leah Doyle have been companions and friends. Oliver Jeffers has provided so much friendship and so many connections; thanks to you and the village of love you share. Raymond Antrobus's friendship and our regular poetry conversations are like a backdrop to the thinking of this book. Gail McConnell's insight and wonder at language, linebreaks, shock and surprise open my eyes to what's happening on the page of a poem. Much of the manuscript was written while living in New York, in the home of Nancy Hechinger, in late 2023 – my thanks to you, Nancy, and the shy horse, for the generosity and kindness. Hearthland – in Kate Capshaw, Steven Spielberg, Rachel Levin and partners – and James Walton, Azita Ardakani Walton, Ben Davis, Sol Guy, and all at Quiet and Civic (Re)Solve have been partners in poetry and peace. My thanks to all involved.

Above all, thanks to the poets – those makers in their lonesome, sometimes lonely, craft – for the work of their language, the detours, delights and devastations from which they've gleaned words for the page, and the permission to include your poems in this book. Thanks to your publishers, and to Fred Courtright at the Permissions Company for sourcing all the permissions. Thanks, too, to Emily Rawling for work and support along the way. I am regularly moved by the attention people give to poetry: thank you to all who've read this book, and previous books, and who contact me, or approach me at conferences or in queues for conversations about poems.

The epigraph that opens the book is from the following source:

Jacques Lacan, excerpt from *Seminar III: The Psychoses 1955–1956*, series ed. Jacques Alain Miller, translated by Russell Grigg. Copyright © 1993 by W. W. Norton & Company, Inc. Used by permission of W. W. Norton & Company, Inc.

The quotation from the seventh chapter of the Letter to the Romans is from David Bentley Hart's translation of The New Testament (Yale University Press, 2017).

Permission Credits

About On Being

Some of the proceeds from the sale of *44 Poems on Being with Each Other* go to support the ongoing work of On Being.

The podcast *Poetry Unbound*, presented by Pádraig Ó Tuama, began in early 2020 and is part of the On Being suite of audio programmes. Each episode is a guided reflection on a single poem.

On Being is a media and public-life initiative, founded and directed by Krista Tippett, an awardee of the 2014 US National Medical for Humanities. On Being takes up the great questions of meaning in twenty-first-century lives and at the intersection of spiritual inquiry, science, social healing, and the arts: *What does it mean to be human? How do we want to live? And who will we be to each other?*

onbeing.org